HOW CHRISTIANITY GROWS IN THE CITY

By Alvin Jennings

[An Expanded Edition of the book, *3 R's of Urban Church Growth*.]

Star

Bible Publications, Inc.
Fort Worth, Texas 76118

— DEDICATION —

To all the saints in Christ Jesus at Boston, Massachusetts, together with the evangelists, overseers and deacons, I dedicate this little volume, *How Christianity Grows In The City.*

It is you above all others of my acquaintance who have effectively implemented the biblical concepts of local church organization, every-member evangelism at home, and world evangelism abroad.

Because you have (1) proven to the present generation that people who have a mind to work for God will be blessed abundantly by Him, and (2) because of your generous commendations of our attempts to express in our first volume some of the ideas you have also found in God's Word and are now practicing so effectively by His power in you, I have been constrained to "thank God and to take new courage."

In devoting one chapter in this second edition to a discussion of what God is doing through you, I am extremely pleased to hold you up as "a model to all the believers" for "the Lord's message rang out from you" and now "your faith in God has become known everywhere" (1 Thess. 1:7-8). Only He knows the extent of triumph He has in store in this great city for His chosen ones.

May it ever be so, is my prayer for you, and may it soon be said of the Lord's Church in hundreds of cities around the earth what we now say concerning you, to the everlasting glory and praise of our blessed Lord Jesus.

FOREWORD
TO THE SECOND EDITION

This book like its predecessor, *3 R's of Urban Church Growth*, is a study in the basics of evangelism and growth of New Testament Christianity in its urban settings.

Reading the Bible is the number one basic. The Bible is the final and only authority in all matters of faith and practice. By *writing* the message and making it plain, men may know how to order their lives (Hab 2:2). Developing skills in writing helps the writer to know his own position and also furnishes a vehicle for communicating to others.

A practice may be practical, but the pragmatist must keep in mind that nothing *really works* or "adds up" if it does not have a biblical base. Our concern will be to calculate what works in our time and place in areas of human judgment, while being careful not to alter the firm foundations of first century doctrines.

Hundreds of letters from across this country and several countries abroad have come in response to this book. There is intense interest in the things about which we speak. One of the main things we hope to accomplish in this edition is to share some of the reactions of readers . . . ranging from "violent" by one brother's own definition, to unreserved commendation on the part of many. One man purchased 100 copies to give away and many others have purchased lesser quantities to share with elders, deacons and other leaders and members of the body of Christ. The most common expression we have heard is, "I have always thought this way, but I never expected any publisher to have the nerve to write it down and distribute it!"

One journalist-friend was so excited when he read it that he offered to re-write it so as to express all controversial subjects so they would be received without offense. We were delighted with the prospect of such an accomplishment by this brother so well-known for his gift in writing. We promptly accepted and offered to acknowledge a shared authorship with him. When he undertook the task, however, he concluded that there was apparently no other way or no better way to convey the thoughts than as they already were written. He did make several suggestions, clarifying expressions that may have been ambiguous or that may be easily misconstrued by anyone seeking for faults. For these suggestions, not only from him, but also from several others, we acknowledge our gratitude and are confident we now have a better second printing because of their help.

We have added four new chapters and an Epilogue in this new edition.

Perhaps the most significant addition will be found in the Epilogue. Here we have given some specific reactions to the book, both negative and positive, and have told of some groups who have used the "one church in a city" concept. We concluded with reviews of books that have recently been published that deal at least in part with the major concerns of this volume.

We pray that the time and effort expended shall be vindicated by a more intense evangelistic spirit among those who read, a much enlarged community of believers in every major city of the world at the earliest possible date, and the ultimate glorification of God, Who would have all true men to be His worshippers in the one body of Jesus Christ (John 4:23-24; Eph. 4:4-6).

Alvin Jennings

March 1, 1985

INTRODUCTION

The growth of the church is a topic which shall never be outmoded, nor will the church ever outgrow a need for considering and reconsidering the subject.

This makes Alvin Jennings' new book appropriate since the growth of the church is the hub of every chapter. He has written this book to help answer the question asked so often, "How do we explain the so far unequalled rapid growth of the church in the first century? What promise do the methods used in the first century hold for a more rapid growth of the church today?"

Brother Jennings draws both from Scripture and secular history as he probes for more light on the church of the first century.

Admittedly some of the conclusions and recommendations in this book are challenging, even revolutionary for the church as it now exists.

The major impact of this book may well be that it will cause exhaustive and detailed re-examination of Scriptures and history so that our view of the early church and her methods may be both clearer and more accurate. Hopefully, the knowledge gained through renewed investigation will lead to better and more extended efforts to spread God's truth everywhere.

— Jule L. Miller

The Great Man . . .

The great man lives in the midst of the multitude essentially alone. His world is their world but he has visions of a better. He rises above his age like a mountain out of a plain. He is the prophet of tomorrow. His contemporaries thus fail to understand him, his thoughts are not their thoughts; his language is not their language. He faces the future. They face the past. He summons them to climb to the heights. They are satisfied with the lowlands. Their world is provincial, his is universal. They worship tradition. He is a devotee of progress.

Carl Trever

Quoted by Bill Teague, Presidential Inaugural Address
Abilene Christian University, Abilene Texas

"Search for truth is the noblest occupation of man; its publication a duty."
— Staël

— CONTENTS —

Reading the Bible — The First Basic In True Religion 1

Communing with God by reading His word is one of the highest forms of worship that man can experience.

In old times God spoke directly with man as He did to Adam,[1] or through the prophets as to Hezekiah through Isaiah,[2] or through the mouth of a dumb beast as to Balaam,[3] or through handwriting on a wall as to King Belshazzar.[4] In these cases, the word of God was "quick and powerful, sharper than any two-edged sword," and pierced to the depths of the thoughts and intents of the hearts of the hearers.[5]

At the end of those days which were recorded in the Old Covenant, God chose to limit His communications to mankind through only one Mediator, His Son.[6] This is a vastly superior way of communication because now when we think we hear a voice in the sky or see a vision in the night, we need not wonder if God is speaking to us. It was perplexing in the old days as to whether it was actually God's voice, or if perhaps it was a deceptive hallucination or imagination. It is not surprising to read how men frequently asked for a sign (a proof) that would assure them of the source of the message.[7]

Now, at the end of these days (the Old Testament era which ended at the cross of Christ[8]), we have a superior law, a superior lawgiver, priest, prophet and king. He is the "one Mediator between God and man;" the One in whom resides all the treasures of heaven and earth, the fulness of the divine godhead, Jesus Christ. It is comforting beyond description that we have received His teaching, His divine last will and testament through the revelation "once for all delivered to the saints."[9] All things that pertain to life and godliness have been delivered through the knowledge of the Son of God in what the Bible calls inspired scripture.[10] It furnishes the man of God completely unto every good work [11] and supplies a pattern for the community of God's people.[12]

A Pattern For God's People

God has given a pattern for His people to follow from Adam to Noah to Moses to Christ. Noah built the ark "according to all that Jehovah commanded him" and Moses built the tabernacle "according to all that Jehovah commanded."[13] These examples serve to the people of God in the Christian dispensation as a solemn warning and admonition that the patterns given to us through Jesus Christ and His special spokesmen, the apostles, be followed explicitly.[14] There must be no adding thereto, no taking away therefrom, nor any changing thereof.[15] The evil consequences of not heeding God's specific instructions are abundant in both the Old and New Testament records, serving as reminders that we dare not handle the word of God negligently, carelessly nor deceitfully.[16]

There seems to be a laxity in our day in properly respecting God's word, the Sacred Scriptures. Many today who profess to be Christ's followers do not read God's word and drink of its message and meanings deeply. The cares of the world and its pleasures crowd out careful Bible study and fervent prayer; the word of God does not "dwell in us richly" in too many cases.[17] Terrible Vision (T.V.) and other worldly allurements have taken our eyes off of things spiritual and robbed Mr. and Mrs. Average Christian of many precious hours of Bible study and faith building.[18]

Blueprint or No Print

The Bible is a blueprint or it is no print at all. It is the last word or it is not God's word. It is the final and only authority in all matters that pertain to religion and morality. A thing is not right because it seems right to man,[19] or because it seems to work and attract a great throng of people. If this be so, then let the Bible be once again chained or burned and let the traditions of Romanism be once again preached to the ignorant masses. Or let the multiplied millions of Communists be cited as proof that "might makes right"! Paul cried out against such pragmatism and popularism when he shouted, "Let God be found true, but every man a liar!"[20]

Faith And Opinion

It is important in ascertaining biblical authority to observe that God has "loosed" some things. That is, He has not given instructions in all matters, but has left them for His people to decide. When the apostles spoke by inspiration they made it clear that whatever was bound upon earth "shall have been bound" in heaven, and whatever was loosed upon earth "shall have been loosed in heaven.[21] Jesus made this distinction to Peter and to the rest of the apostles. We have chosen to give the literal translation from the Greek rather than the translation appearing in the common English versions so that the significance of the *order* or *source* might be seen. Heaven did not bind or loose whatever the apostles spoke, but rather the apostles spoke only those things that had already been established as bound or loosed in heaven. Peter stated the same truth in his epistle when he wrote that no scripture is of any private interpretation (more correctly, it does not emanate or originate from the impulse or whim of man), but holy men spake as they were moved by the Spirit of God. The subject here is not how the scriptures are received and understood, but rather how they originated or were "brought forth" as is noted in the marginal reading of the A.S.V.[22]

When God through His inspired prophets or apostles "bound" baptism (Greek, immersion), it had already been established in heaven. From this there can be no deviation or alteration. This is a matter of faith that comes from hearing the word of God.[23] However, the apostles did *not* bind that immersion be in a natural body of water such as a river or lake. Since this was left "loosed" by the apostles, it therefore is left to the convenience or opinion of men as to whether persons be baptized in natural bodies of water or in man-made pools. Wherever the scripture has not bound, disciples are at liberty to exercise their opinion according to their best wisdom or understanding of the circumstances at hand. It is therefore immaterial whether the 3,000 souls on Pentecost were immersed in the Pool of Siloam or in a nearby natural stream outside the city gates. Such matters of human opinion are to be regulated by a sense of what is appropriate, decent and orderly,[24] and no man should make any laws or bind restrictions not given by God. All things should be done in a spirit of love and peace.

Conclusion

Putting these principles together, we conclude that we can obey God and have peace and harmony among ourselves as servants of God if we remember a simple slogan from the pioneer American, Thomas Campbell, who said:

> In matters of faith, unity
> In matters of opinion, liberty
> In all things, charity.[25]

We believe these principles read from the word of God are as fundamental in true religion as the 3 R's in the schoolroom, as basic as meat and potatoes on the dining table or as basic as blocking and tackling in the game of football. With these preliminaries in mind, we are prepared to begin our voyage. We shall read in the next chapter about the Jerusalem community of believers, its growth and the treasure of implications for us today.

QUESTIONS

1. How did God speak to the fathers in the former times before Christ?

2. How many mediators do we have today between God and us? Who?

3. What passage shows the Bible to be a blueprint or a pattern?

4. What is the significance of distinguishing between matters of faith and opinion in religion?

5. Give the meaning of "no scripture is of private interpretation" (2 Peter 1:20-21).

FOOTNOTES

1 Genesis 1-3
2 Isaiah 38
3 Numbers 22
4 Daniel 5
5 Hebrews 4:12
6 Hebrews 1:1-2
7 Judges 6:37-39
8 1 Timothy 2:5; Hebrews 1-2; Colossians 2:9
9 Jude 3; Hebrews 9:15-17
10 2 Peter 1:3
11 2 Timothy 3:16-17
12 Hebrews 8:5
13 Genesis 6:5; Exodus 39:32
14 1 Corinthians 10:11; Romans 15:4
15 Revelation 22:18-19; Galatians 1:8-9
    1 Corinthians 4:6; 2 John 9-11
16 Leviticus 10:1-2; Acts 5:1-11
17 Colossians 3:16-17; Luke 8:13-14
18 Romans 10:17; 2 Timothy 2:15
19 Isaiah 55:8-9; Proverbs 14:12
20 Romans 3:4
21 Matthew 16:18; 18:18
22 2 Peter 1:20-21; also cf 1 Corinthians 11:23
23 Romans 10:17
24 1 Corinthians 14:33, 40
25 *Declaration And Address, 1809 A.D.*

Jerusalem, The First Urban Community of Christians

2

I n reviewing the beginning and growth of the first church of Christ in Jerusalem, we will be observing basics in all areas of *"readin, ritin,* and *rithmetic"!* The writer Luke continued his inspired narrative addressed to Theophilus so that he and all who read would have an accurate chronological history. Although numbers do not tell the whole story, the arithmetic of the first chapters of the book of Acts is prominent in the record.

In Mark 16:15 Jesus instructed the apostles to go into all the world and preach the gospel to every creature. Such a command to only eleven men seemed incredible! But not only did they survive, but they accepted the challenge and they actually spread the gospel to the whole world. The pattern of growth was outlined by the Holy Spirit in Acts 1:8; first in Jerusalem, then to the province of Judea, thence northward to Samaria and finally to the whole world during their lifetime.[1]

Notice the numerous mathematical terms used to describe the rapid growth of the Jerusalem church:

1. About 3,000 souls "added to them"   2:41
2. "The Lord added day by day those that were saved."   2:47
3. "The number of men came to about 5,000"   4:4
   The estimated total number including the

16

women and single persons would be approximately 12,000 souls.

4. "Believers were the more added to the Lord, multitudes both of men and women." 5:14

5. "The number was multiplying." 6:1

6. "And the word of God increased; and the number of the disciples multiplied in Jerusalem exceedingly; and a great company of the priests were obedient to the faith." 6:7

In the early days, at least one was baptized per day (2:47) — an absolute minimum of 365 per year. When the terms "multiplied," "the more added," "multiplying," "increased," "multiplied exceedingly," and "great company" are used, there is no way to determine how many Christians there may have been in this city by the time the book of Acts was ended. According to the estimates of various scholars, the Jerusalem congregation had a membership of between 50,000 and 100,000. Notice the biblical emphasis on the "arithmetics" of the church's growth.

Before the end of their generation, those who started with so few grew until the message had spread to the known world.[2] The enemies became alarmed and by A.D. 50 they said that Christians had "turned the world upside down."[3] About the same time, Paul quoted Psalms 19:5 and applied it to his day: "Yea, verily, their sound went out into all the earth, and their words unto the ends of the world."[4]

Places of Assembly

Christians were teaching daily in the Temple courtyard area.[5] They also taught in homes and prayed and had meals of fellowship together.[6] They "came to their own company" ("group," T.S.B.), possibly to a home, where they lifted their voices in a prayer of thanksgiving and praise to God after the release of Peter and John from prison.[7]

The multitude of disciples was called together by the

twelve[8] but we are not told where the place of meeting was nor how the word was spread to the multitude of Christians.

When the persecution against the church in Jerusalem arose, "Saul laid waste the church, entering into every house" and dragged men and women out and committed them to prison.[9] It is evident that the church met in the homes of disciples from whence the persecutors dragged them, possibly even during meetings.

Organization

God set apostles and prophets (inspired teachers) in the church,[10] and also evangelists, pastors and teachers.[11] The first record we have of a specific mention of elders is chapter 11:29-30, then again reference is made to them in 15:6, 22. Special servants (sometimes called deacons) were chosen to minister to the needs of widows.[12] The apostles received and distributed funds from some place known to be their place of functioning.[13] The group at Jerusalem (church) heard and sent Barnabas;[14] they were consulted by the brethren from Antioch.[15] The place or office where they met together is not designated, though it possibly was where prayer was constantly made at Mary's house.[16] The elders congregated at some unspecified place to greet Paul after his missionary journey.[17] Philip Schaff concludes: "They went daily to the Temple to teach, as their Master had done, but held their devotional meetings in private houses (2:46; 3:1; 5:42)."[18]

QUESTIONS

1. What does the word "church" mean to you?

2. How many members of the Jerusalem church were there at the end of the day of Pentecost?

3. What is the highest numerical count given in the Book of Acts for the Jerusalem disciples? What is the figure given by scholars later on?

4. Was Jerusalem ever "filled" with the doctrine (teaching) of Christ?

5. Give your ideas concerning the place(s) of assembly of the Jeru-

salem church.

6. Is there any distinctive "office" in the Jerusalem church that no other church had?

FOOTNOTES

[1] Colossians 1:6, 23
[2] Colossians 1:23, AD 61
[3] Acts 17:6
[4] Romans 10:18
[5] Acts 2:46; 5:20,25,28
[6] Acts 2:46; 5:42
[7] Acts 4:23,31
[8] Acts 6:2,5
[9] Acts 8:1-3
[10] Ephesians 4:11
[11] 1 Corinthians 12:28
[12] Acts 6. Ron Smotherman and James Bales concur in their extensive studies on "diakonos" that these who served in Acts 6 were probably not serving in the official functionary sense as Paul later used this term.
[13] Acts 5:1-2, 14; 8:3, 14
[14] Acts 9:26, 28; 11:22
[15] Acts 15:2,4,6,22,23
[17] Acts 21:17-19
[18] *History of the Christian Church*, Vol. I, p. 248

Christianity Grows When Christians Are Added

3

No study on the growth of Christianity could be complete without a precise biblical definition of what a Christian is and a clear description of the process by which a person becomes a Christian. The growth rate of Christianity in any city would be a measurement of the increase of the number of disciples in that place. God adds to His church all those who are saved (Acts 2:47) and thus the church, the body of Christ, grows.

Are You A Christian?

Every person in the world should be asked, "Are **you** a Christian?" And everyone deserves to have a true Bible definition of what a Christian is, and how to become one. The apostle Paul wanted all people to become Christians. Some were persuaded to be what Paul was, and some were not. One man said, "Almost thou persuadest me to become a Christian" (Acts 26:28). The word "Christian" appears only three times in the Bible, and this is one of them (the others are Acts 11:26 and 1 Peter 4:16).

Answers Some People Give

For several years, I have made it a practice to ask people that I meet, "Are you a Christian?" It is obvious that very few people in the "Christian" nation of America have a biblical concept of what a Christian is. Listen to these answers.

I asked a young man at a gasoline service station, "Are you a Christian?" His reply: "I don't know if I am or not." After thinking for a moment he added with a smile, "I suppose a Christian would go to church, but I don't believe going to church would necessarily mean a person is a Christian."

Another was Yolanda, a waitress. When she pondered the question she said, "I believe a Christian is a person you can trust."

On another occasion, I was in a clothing store. While the store manager was writing up the ticket, I asked him: "Sir, are you a Christian?" He was a handsome young oriental man, and might have been expected to answer negatively. He said, "I am a Catholic. Does that count?"

Then there was Pam, a young woman about 25 years of age, in California. She replied, "Yes, sir, I am a Christian. I was baptized a long time ago and went to a Christian church in Houston." She had already told about living with her fiance three years and of her plans to get married.

Now let me tell you about talking with a boy named Phil, age 19: "Are you a Christian, Phil?" "No, I'm a Baptist. I believe in God but I don't go to church. I don't get anything out of just sitting there. My parents made me go when I was a boy." He seemed confused and sorrowful as he reflected on his family and his present frustration and aimlessness in life.

How different the above from the telephone salesman, who was asked the same question: "Yes, I am a Christian," he replied. "I am an ordained Baptist preacher. I realize that although the name Baptist Church is not in the Bible, it is nevertheless an organization of Christians to get the gospel preached."

Another said, "I believe in God but I haven't been to

church for over a year. I don't know if I am a Christian or not." His countenance was fallen and he spoke in very low tones, obviously confused.

When I see people who are strangers, I try to view them as made in God's image, and remember that God wants all men to become His worshippers (John 4:23). Almost all who are asked if they are a Christian seem concerned and courteous and appreciative of my interest and they seem to try to give an honest reply. Some have been frank to admit that they do not know what makes a person a Christian. A few seemed to feel as if their ignorance of God's commands will somehow excuse them and get them by. But that is not true according to Acts 17:30-31:

> The times of ignorance therefore God overlooked; but now he commandeth men everywhere to repent: inasmuch as he hath appointed a day in which he will judge the world in righteousness by the man whom he hath ordained; whereof he hath given assurance unto all men, in that he hath raised him from the dead.

In the old days before Christ came to the world, a heathen man could be ignorant of God's law and still be saved if he followed whatever law he had and if by seeing the great manifestations in nature such as the wonders of animal and plant life and all creation, he would admit there is a Great Creator God above all the earth (see Romans 1:18-32). It is obvious, however, that no one could have known how to become a Christian before Christ Himself came to the earth and taught men about Himself.

Space does not allow us to give more examples of what people have said in response to the question, "Are you a Christian?" We can summarize the categories of their answers in the following way:

"Yes, I am a Methodist" (or any denomination).

"No, I do not go to church anywhere."

"Yes, I'm an American and this is a Christian nation."

"Yes, my mother was a Christian so I suppose that

makes me one too."

"Yes, I treat my neighbor fair and I pay my taxes and take care of my family, so I am a Christian."

Some may be difficult to understand like the doctor who was asked if he considered himself to be a Christian: he replied, "I hope I am — most of the time —!"

If each of these replies is examined, it will be seen that all have not given God's definition, and perhaps none has. One may feel it is following some popular religion and attending a church regularly. Another feels it is something like politics that you have inherited as a good citizen of this country. And yet another assumes identity as a Christian is passed from parent to child like blue eyes or dark hair. Some people feel that if they do the things Christians ought to do from day to day in living a good moral life, that they must have at some mysterious point in their life become a Christian. This is like those who assume that if they act like married people act, that they have somehow entered into the state of matrimony along the way! (In truth, they are living in adultery rather than in matrimony.) It is one thing to *get* married, and another to act like you're married. It is one thing to *become* a Christian, and another to act like a Christian.

Would "going to church" and sitting in a church building make you a Christian, any more than sitting in a chicken house would make you a chicken? Of course not.

What Really Is A Christian?

Since many conflicting opinions are given when the question is considered, let us turn to the Bible and let God speak. At exactly what point and by what means does a person leave the condition or state of being an "outsider", "heathen", or a "child of Satan"? When does he enter the different and glorious life with God which the Scriptures refer to as being a disciple of Christ? When and how does this new life begin?

A Christian Would Eagerly
Hear The Word Of God — But Hearing Alone
Does Not Make A Person A Christian

Hearing the good news of salvation from sin and death, and of eternal happiness in heaven and of all the other grand and marvelous doctrines of the Bible, will richly bless the heart of the person who listens and receives it gladly (Luke 8:8,11,15). Hearing God's Word will produce faith (Romans 10:17):

> So belief *cometh* of hearing, and hearing by the word of Christ.

But hearing without doing is to act like a fool who builds his house upon the sand (Matthew 7:24-27):

> Every one therefore that heareth these words of mine, and doeth them, shall be likened unto a wise man, who built his house upon the rock; and the rain descended, and the floods came, and the winds blew, and beat upon that house; and it fell not: for it was founded upon the rock. And every one that heareth these words of mine, and doeth them not, shall be likened unto a foolish man, who built his house upon the sand; and the rain descended, and the floods came, and the winds blew, and smote upon that house; and it fell: and great was the fall thereof.

All Christians hear and read the Word of God but there is much more to becoming a Christian than merely listening to or reading the Bible.

A Christian Would Believe In God
And In His Son, Jesus Christ —
But Believing Alone Does Not Make A Person
A Christian

"Without faith it is impossible to please God" states Hebrews 11:6. When a person receives faith by hearing the gospel of Christ (Romans 10:17) that gives him the right to move ahead and become a son of God (John 1:11-12).

> He came unto his own, and they that were his own received him not. But as many as received him, to them

gave he the right to become children of God, *even* to them that believe on his name.

Many who believe in Jesus are not Christians. They are unwilling to exercise the right or the power to move ahead and act and become a Christian, a child of God. A specific case of this is found in John 12:42 where it is stated that many believed even of the rulers of the people but their faith was to no avail because they feared the people more than they loved the glory of God, and were unwilling to openly confess their faith. Other passages that show the barrenness and insufficiency of faith alone are Galatians 5:6 and James 2:14-26. We must conclude therefore that all Christians believe in Jesus Christ as the Son of God, but not all who believe are Christians. There is a faith that saves, and there is a faith that is barren and does not save. Even the devils believe but surely no one would say that they are Christians (James 2:19-20):

> Thou believest that God is one; thou doest well: the demons also believe, and shudder. But wilt thou know, O vain man, that faith apart from works is barren?

Here is an example from the world to show that it takes somebody who not only believes, but who is also willing to sacrifice to accomplish the goal. The story is told of Elizabeth Blackwell who was the first woman doctor in America. She began her practice in 1851 in New York. People were prejudiced against her. No hospital would allow her on their staff. She was unable to get any patients, and no one would even rent her a room once she told them she was a doctor.

Finally, with the help of some Quaker friends, she opened her own clinic in New York City's worst slum. The clinic began in March, 1853. She put out a sign saying that treatment would be free, yet for weeks no one came. But one day a woman staggered up the steps, collapsed in Elizabeth's arms, was treated and recovered. She returned to tell her friends about "the wonderful woman doctor." The clinic eventually expanded into what is now New York Infirmary for Women and Children, a large thriving hospital on East 15th Street in New York City. Her faith and sacrificial spirit made it a reality.

A Christian Is One Who Has Decided To Cease Living In Sin — But Living A Pure, Moral Life Is Not Assurance That One Is A Christian

Jesus charged, "Except you repent, you shall all in like manner perish" (Luke 13:3,5). God commands all men everywhere to repent (Acts 17:30) and to turn away from the works of the flesh that war against the soul. Many people who do not believe in Jesus Christ live pure, moral lives. Those who practice Hinduism and Shintoism are for the most part good citizens and good moral family people. Other people sometimes turn away from sin because its rewards are bitter and painful even when there is no religious motivation of any kind. Look at the changed life of the former alcoholic or dope addict. Some who were criminals quit their life of crime because of a fear of getting caught and being punished by the civil authorities, and yet they may not profess to be religious at all.

A Christian is to turn away from every form of sin just like Joseph fled away from evil in Egypt, but a pure moral life is not in itself evidence that one is in Christ and worthy of the name "Christian". Cornelius is a good example of a man that was not only of an excellent moral character, but he was also very religious. However, he was not a Christian until he heard the words of salvation from Peter (see Acts 10), believed and obeyed Jesus Christ.

Repentance is the most difficult part of becoming a Christian. It is the resolution to change and to say in your heart, "I will pay whatever price it costs to do what my Lord requires of me." It may mean changing one's complete lifestyle, his job, his habits, his conversation, his entertainment, his companions, and perhaps the form of religion once held. The rich ruler of Mark 10:17-22 is a prime example of one who heard and believed in Jesus, but who was not willing to make the sacrifice of changing his way of life.

A Christian Is One Who Tells Others Of His Faith — But Not All Who Merely Make Professions With Their Mouths Are True Christians

Jesus spoke of some as hypocrites who honored him "with their lips but their heart is far from me" (Matthew 15:7-9 quoting Isaiah 29:13).

> Ye hypocrites, well did Isaiah prophesy of you, saying, This people honoreth me with their lips; But their heart is far from me. But in vain do they worship me, Teaching *as their* doctrines the precepts of men.

They professed with their speech to be followers of God's law, while in religious practice they were actually following the doctrines and commandments of men. Jesus exposed the hypocrisy of false prophets on another occasion as seen in Matthew 7:15-23 where some were calling him "Lord" and yet were not obeying the will of the Father in heaven:

> Beware of false prophets, who come to you in sheep's clothing, but inwardly are ravening wolves. By their fruits ye shall know them. Do *men* gather grapes of thorns, or figs of thistles? Even so every good tree bringeth forth good fruit; but the corrupt tree bringeth forth evil fruit. A good tree cannot bring forth evil fruit, neither can a corrupt tree bring forth good fruit. Every tree that bringeth not forth good fruit is hewn down, and cast into the fire. Therefore by their fruits ye shall know them. Not every one that saith unto me, Lord, Lord, shall enter into the kingdom of heaven; but he that doeth the will of my Father who is in heaven. Many will say to me in that day, Lord, Lord, did we not prophesy by thy name, and by thy name cast out demons, and by thy name do many mighty works? And then will I profess unto them, I never knew you: depart from me, ye that work iniquity.

Yes, a Christian will confess Jesus Christ before men (Matthew 10:32-33; Romans 10:9-10), but not all who do so are Christians. The Judgment Day will be a day of great surprises for many who make loud speeches and long prayers in the name of Christ. There they will hear Him say, "Depart from me, ye cursed, into the eternal fire which is prepared for the devil and his angels" (Matthew 25:41-46).

A Christian Is One Who Has Been Baptized — But Not All Who Have Been Baptized Are Christians

In Romans chapter six, we read of the beautiful way you and I can become identified with Jesus Christ in His death, His burial and His resurrection:

Beginning with verse 3:
Or are ye ignorant that all we who were baptized into Christ Jesus were baptized into his death? We were buried therefore with him through baptism into death: that like as Christ was raised from the dead through the glory of the Father, so we also might walk in newness of life.

This burial is in water (Acts 8:36; 10:47). It is the time when God by Jesus' blood washes away our sins (Acts 22:16). However, if this act is not obeyed sincerely from the heart, then going through this formality becomes merely a sham, a pretense and a mockery in the sight of God (Romans 6:17-18):

But thanks be to God, that whereas ye were servants of sin ye became obedient from the heart to that form of teaching whereunto ye were delivered; and being made free from sin, ye became servants of righteousness.

Thus, not all who are immersed are Christians.

Some infants are made to participate in a ceremony called "baptism" which is an unbiblical doctrine. Being sprinkled or poured as an infant cannot take the place of obeying from the heart that form of doctrine spoken of in Romans chapter six. Nor is being immersed in water of any value if it is for the wrong purpose, such as to "show the world that God has saved you." In these ways it is seen that not all those who have experienced something called baptism are Christians.

Unfortunately, there are some who believe in God and live good lives, even worship God and confess His name, and yet who have never obeyed their Lord by being buried in the watery grave of baptism. They just keep delaying, putting it off until a more convenient time. How tragic when sometimes a good man or woman just waits too long, and then goes down to the grave unprepared to meet God . . . still not quite in the kingdom, not quite a Christian, just outside the door.

Added To The Body

By obeying the gospel in this fashion, a person becomes a Christian and enters into the body of Christ which is His church (Acts 2:47; Colossians 1:18):

Acts 2:47
. . . praising God, and having favor with all the people. And the Lord added to them day by day those that were saved.
Colossians 1:18
And he is the head of the body, the church: who is the beginning, the firstborn from the dead; that in all things he might have the preeminence.

This church is referred to in the Bible as "the church of the Lord" (Acts 20:28) and by many other descriptive names and phrases (see pages 97 - 103 for a full discussion on names). He then is born again and begins to walk a new life in Christ Jesus, and must continue faithful unto death if he would receive the reward in heaven.

Are You A Christian?

With these clear first principles from the Bible well in mind, would you answer that being a Catholic "counts" as being a Christian? Or that if a person is a member of a certain church or denomination, though not mentioned in the Bible, that he is a Christian? Or that if an individual fills a pew in some church house every Sunday, that this would prove that he is the family of God's saved ones, that he is a Christian?

QUESTIONS

1. Who does Jesus describe as a fool in Matthew 7:24-27?

2. Will faith alone save?

3. Can you give a definition of "repent"?

4. Does God accept all who honor Him with their lips?

5. Describe how a person may be buried with Jesus Christ into His death.

6. Is baptism necessary in order to receive forgiveness of sins?

7. Tell the relationship between people being saved and church growth.

8. Can you give examples of confusion as to what a Christian is?

Note: The contents of this chapter is published in a separate booklet. Write to the publisher for information.

Meeting Places
Of Early
Christians   4

"Come Tell Us In What Places You Assemble"

The church met in the homes of disciples according to the record in Acts and in the epistles. Their devotions through prayer, reading, singing, etc. were in private houses, and occasionally public gatherings of the saints would be found in the Temple area in Jerusalem. Various historians give from fifty thousand to one hundred thousand as the estimated number of Christians in that city alone before the close of the first century, leaving no doubt but that homes were utilized for regular Lord's Day meetings. The growth was so rapid, rising from three thousand to over five thousand men (besides women) in a very short time, it would have been virtually impossible to have accomodated the throngs any other way.

The New Testament contains very little information about the meeting places of the *ekklesia,* the church. This word denoted the place of assembly in later times, but in Acts and the Epistles there is no *local* significance, as of a place or a building. It meant only the congregation of the faithful. The espistle of James (2:2) mentions an assembly. The word used is "synagogue," an anglicized Greek word meaning "to come together."

Some suppose that the use of this word suggests the synagogue was used as a disciples' meeting house. Some of them were large and imposing structures, and it is obvious that the early Christians neither desired nor were able to erect buildings of the character of these legally sanctioned buildings. Some have supposed that the early Christians used the synagogue to meet in before their final separation from the Jews. However, in cities where a sizable number of Jews became obedient to the faith, the hostility was sharp between the Jewish leaders and the Christians who converted their 'flock', which would have prevented their use of the synagogue. We have found no historical evidence that Christians used the synagogues.

Since Christianity was cradled in Jerusalem, the Temple was long held sacred by many converts and they continued to assemble there at "the hour of prayer." One of its porticoes they chose for a time as their place of daily assembly.[1]

In the book, *Acts of Martyrdom,* dated in the second century, Justin Martyr refers to the meetings of Christians in private homes. When the Christians were brought up before the Prefect of Rome, they were asked, "Where do you assemble?" To this Justin replied:

> "Where each one chooses and can; do you suppose that we all are accustomed to meet together in one place? Quite otherwise, for the God of the Christians is not confined by place, but being invisible, He fills the heaven and the earth, and the faithful everywhere adore Him and sing His praise."

The Prefect repeats the charge, "Come tell us in what place you assemble and gather your followers?"[2]

> In the first Apology of Justin, Chapter 67, Justin wrote:
> "And on the day called Sunday, all who live in cities or in the country gather together to one place and the memoirs of the apostles or the writings of the prophets are read as long as time permits."

He goes on to describe the Lord's Supper without further reference to the place.

These meetings in private houses did not pass out of use when Christianity became a more public institution. The custom remained in vogue up until freedom of religion was proclaimed by Constantine, and legacies were permitted to be received by the church. This provided abundant funds for church buildings, but the custom of meeting in private homes still seemed to remain.

The arrangement of the ancient houses was two-fold: (1) the normal house in the country where there was freedom of space, and (2) the city residences where crowded conditions prevailed and where upper stories were constructed. This is what accounts for the expression "upper room" which occurs several times in the scripture. When one of these fine residences was willed to a church, it usually became a center for Christian life and work for the town and surrounding country.

The invention of religious objects is curious. The lamps and candelabra which figure so largely show that meetings were held in the evening or before dawn. Another item of interest was a group of cups or chalices, used for the Lord's Supper. And always an abundant supply of men's and women's garments were kept in store. These garments were to be worn while dining at the Love Feast banquets (something like a wedding garment). This gave a sense of equality for the poorer and the richer to feel as "one."

Immediately after the crucifixion, the apostles met behind closed doors "for fear of the Jews," and later throughout the book of Acts it is clear they and the disciples met specifically for prayers and devotions only in the private homes of fellow Christians. The atmosphere of one meeting of this kind is recaptured from the account of Paul's visit at Troas (Acts 20:7-8), possibly a rented hall of some size ("many lights"), or an upper chamber in a private dwelling.

No "Church-house" of the first century has ever been discovered. It would not be recognizable if it were, where a room or rooms were set aside expressly for this purpose. The earliest of these recognized were at Dura on the Euphrates and in Lullingstone Park near Eynsford in Kent.

The one at Kent, built before 250 A.D., has rooms for instruction, a place for baptism and the Lord's Supper. It consisted originally of two rooms which were later converted into a single rectangular hall with a raised platform at the narrow east end. This is the sole survivor of this kind. The minister's quarters were upstairs. Baptistries became a part of the more elaborate house-churches, as is supposed from wall paintings of Jesus' baptism in Jordan and of Philip's baptism of the Ethiopian.[3]

The custom of meeting in private homes continued down through the end of persecutions. After that, their use was discouraged on the basis that meetings should not be conducted without the oversight of the church authorities. It was held that they would lead to deviations of various kinds from orthodox practice and teaching. They were prohibited unless licensed especially by the Bishop.[4]

The only examples of church-owned edifices that have survived from the first three centuries of Christianity provide striking evidence of the difference in conditions before and after its adoption by the Roman State as the new religion.

Eusebius tells us that there were 46 presbyters at Rome in the middle of the third century. Optatus also informs there were more than 40 Roman basilicas, suggesting there were that number of separate congregations, each presided over by a presbyter. Did they only meet in private homes? Probably not. At some parts of the city common meeting places not connected with the private houses had been erected at an early period.

These modest halls (like the colleges and clubs used) were likely procured or erected, purposely resembling the plain buildings of the Schole (fraternity or lodge rooms) so as to avoid persecutions. These structures frequently were connected to burial grounds.

When the emperior Constantine came to the throne (307-337 A.D.), he was eager to provide buildings for Christians equal in magnificance to the old basilicas and temples. He built 7 in Rome (at least), and others in Italian cities, in Africa, Syria, and Asia.

Krautheimer has indicated what kind of space was needed. A large assembly room, an anteroom for cate-chumens and penitents, classrooms, a dining room for the agape, storerooms and living quarters.[7] In the first and second centuries Christians had met in houses. In the third century they still did so, but now they had taken over entire houses, often large, and had remodeled them for church use. Near the city wall of Eura-Europus on the Euphrates was a Jewish community house and close by, a Christian community house as well. The former building was adapted for Jewish use around 200 and completely rebuilt in 245; the latter was remodeled for Christian use in 231. Both were destroyed in 257 when the wall was reinforced against Persian attack.[8]

In spite of their considerable size the Christian community houses were relatively inconspicuous, and only occasionally did outsiders enter and threaten worshippers with arrest. Tertullian, describing the life of Christians in the world, argues that they are just like everyone else.[9]

Deacons, supposed to administer the church's funds well, were actually dipping into them in order to grow rich from funds given for charitable purposes.[10] Presbyters were engaged in business,[11] and bishops bequeathed their sees to relatives and friends, sometimes paying for popular votes.[12]

At Antioch Paul of Samosata apparently held title to

"house of the church."[13] It would appear, however, that the bishop ordinarily delegated control, and perhaps title, in the third century. *The Apostolic Tradition of Hippolytus* describes the deacon as ordained by the bishop alone and for his service; the deacon's function is to take charge of church property.[14] In the early third century church properties were held in the names of deacons, chosen to represent the bishops. The deacons were thus in a position to confuse church funds with their own, as Origen says they did. But since ultimate control rested with the bishop, bishops themselves could try to bequeath churches by will, as Origen again says they did. The title to church properties when held by bishops and deacons made it expressively easy for these officers to mix up church funds with their own — as Hippolytus and Origen say they did.[15]

Porphyry criticized the practice, claiming that Christians "were erecting very large houses, resembling temples, for their worship; they could just as well have prayed at home."[16]

In 321 Constantine insisted that property could be left by will to "the most holy and venerable council [concilium] of the Catholic church," presumably with individual churches in view.[17]

The first account we have of any action of Christians in acquiring of land, presumably for erecting a building, suggests a schola. It happened during the time of Alexander Severus (222-235 A.D.), and was disputed by tavern keepers who also wanted the space for their trade.

Many of the Roman basilicas are outside the walls of the ancient cities. The two most notable are St. Peter's on the Vatican and St. Paul's on the road to Ostia. These churches originated neither in private homes nor in the lodge-rooms, but in the memorial cellae of the martyrs whose bones supposedly rested beneath them. At first these were simple chapels, but ever increasing throngs visited them and they grew by the fifth century to enormous "churches." The proximity of the martyr's grave to the church building was of great importance — a feeling that a church altar was hallowed by contact with the body or relic of a saint. When the building was reconstructed or enlarged, special care was taken by the architects to avoid changing the situation of the altar in its relation to the sacred tomb.

Buildings used by early Christians had several root-fibers traceable back to non-Christian origins from the age of Constantine. There was first the synagogue, a place of affection for all Jewish converts, that offered a model in many ways for the meetinghouse of the brethren. The primitive Christians assembled when and where they best could, exposed from time to time to molestation. Could it have been to encourage the brethren that Revelation 21:22 describes the New Jerusalem as dispensing with any visible shrine or building needed for prayer?

As the rivalry developed with the Jewish religion, Christians separated from the synagogues, and met in private dwellings or in some places a hall was rented or constructed, called a lodge-hall or schola. This was the earliest form of church building. These were merely buildings for accomodation; that is to say, there was no connection between the feeling of the Christian community and the architectural features of its buildings. All they sought was needful shelter and privacy arranged on a convenient plan.

It was not until the memorial *cella* of the cemeteries were constructed that an architecture of an expressive kind was begun, erected not so much for *use* as for *feeling,* for the celebration of an idea which the community had at heart, the commemoration of its mighty martyrs. Eusebius calls them "Trophies of the Martyrs," evidently meaning some conspicuous monument above ground, an *exedra* or *cella.*

Although the age of Constantine is generally regarded

as the beginning date of the church as an "institution," considerable light is thrown upon church buildings as early as half a century earlier. Eusebius refers to forty years peace of the church which preceded the Diocletian persecution in A.D. 303. He writes:

"Innumerable multitudes of men flocked daily to the religion of Christ."

"Illustrious concourse of people in the sacred edifices. . ."

". . . no longer content with the ancient buildings, they erected spacious churches from the foundation in all the cities."[18]

These "spacious" buildings were referred to by the emperor Aurelian (270-275 A.D.) indicating they were well-known features in Roman cities. All these were destroyed by edict of Diocletian: "Tear down the sacred buildings to the foundation, and burn the Holy Scriptures with fire." None of the remains exist today.[19]

On the carved sarcophagi and in the mosaic pictures of the period after Constantine, occur representations of the church building of that day. In these pictures baptistries are seen (round side structures), fourth century.

Church architecture's monumental history therefore has its beginning at the age of Constantine, when an entirely new era was introduced for the church. For the first time Christianity was placed openly under the protection of the law and the important right of receiving legacies was accorded it. Constantine became interested in ecclesiastical affairs and gave the church the prestige of imperial favor. The church responded at once and surrounded itself with the utmost possible pomp and splendor. Squared and heavy stone structures replaced the light buildings recently destroyed, and "temples rose once more from the soil to a lofty height, and received a splendour far exceeding that which had been formerly destroyed . . . throughout all the cities."[20]

QUESTIONS

1. What is the meaning of the Greek word transliterated "synagogue"?

2. Did meetings in private houses pass out of use when Christianity was adopted as the official religion of the Roman empire?

3. What was the single most significant factor in the beginning of churches owning community property?

4. What was the *schola* ?

5. What was the *Cella* ?

6. Was Diocletian favorable to Christianity and church edifices?

FOOTNOTES

[1] Acts 3:1
[2] Ruinart, Octa Martyrum Sincera, Ratisbon, 1859, p. 106 (Acts of Martyrdom)
[3] cf, Clementine, Recognitions, IV. 6
[4] p. 47, Brown ibid
[5] Gough, p. 58 ff.
[6] Jones, p. 90
[7] R. Krautheimer, Early Christian and Byzantine Architecture (Baltimore, 1965), 5.
[8] For the church see M.I. Rostovtzeff, ed., The Excavations at Dura-

Europos: Preliminary Report of Fifth Season of Work (New Haven, 1934), 238-88; C.H. Kraeling, The Excavations at Dura-Europos: Final Report, VIII, Part 2: The Christian Building (Locust Valley, NY, 1967). Also published at New Haven, Dura-Europos Publications, 1967.

[9] Tertullian, Apol. 43, 1-3; cf. Ad Diognetum 5.

[10] Ibid., 16, 22.

[11] Ezek. hom, 7.

[12] Num, hom. 22, 4.

[13] Eusebius, H.E. 7, 30, 19.

[14] Apost. Trad. 9, 1-2 (presumably against Callistus).

[15] Bishops who withdrew from their sees in times of persecution pre- left control of properties in the hands of their deacons.

[16] Ibid., 8, 1, 5: Prophyry, Frag. 76 Harnack.

[17] Cod. Theod. 16, 2, 4; cf. Kaser, op cit., 348; H. Dorries, Das Selbstzeugnis Kaiser Konstantis (Gottingen, 1954), 183.

[18] Hist. Eccl. viii, 1, Eusebius

[19] Ibid., viii, 2.

[20] Ibid., x, 2, 3.

Above works cited in the following principle sources:

G. Galdwin Brown
From Schola To Cathedral, Edinburgh 1886, 231 pp.
(Chapter on Places of Meeting, pages 33-74)

Michael Gough
The Early Christians, Frederick A. Praeger, NY 1961

R. M. Grant
Augustus to Constantine, Harper & Row, NY & London, 1970
Chapter, The Buildings and Finds, pp. 173-178

Our Faith
And Our
Traditions

5

Jesus made a distinction between some things that are essential and necessary, and other things that are of secondary concern, though useful.

Some examples of this in His ministry were the relative values of (1) a garment and its patch, (2) wine and the container, and (3) taking time for listening to Him as compared to time spent in household duties.[1]

To make these distinctions is of great importance in the everyday life of the church. In the cases cited above, the fresh, the new, the divine, the true stand out above the old, the human, the physical. The wine represents the new, the real substance; the wineskins represent the secondary concern, necessary but only serving in a supporting role.

And he spake also a parable unto them: No man rendeth a piece from a new garment and putteth it upon an old garment; else he will rend the new, and also the piece from the new will not agree with the old. And no man putteth new wine into old wine-skins; else the new wine will burst the skins, and itself will be spilled, and the skins will perish. But new wine must be put into fresh wine-skins. **Luke 5:36-38**

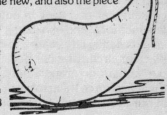

The gospel itself is the ever-new yet changeless life-giving source and strength; the container or wineskin represents the forms, the habits or traditional ways people have been doing things. These latter things are important because they actually serve as the point of contact between the church and the world, and they must be determined by the properties of the wine (the gospel) and the conditions and pressures of the world on the outside.

The Pharisees were troubled when they saw Jesus' disciples did not conform to their fathers' traditions . . . to the habits and rituals which, though not a part of the law, had assumed a rigid and changeless part of religious practice enforced by the Rabbis. Jesus knew they were irritated because His disciples did not obey all their customs. Their concern for whether the disciples fasted or not was really not their problem. They were bothered because their human forms and traditions were at stake. As they stated in Matthew 15:2, "Why do your disciples transgress the tradition of the elders?"

Jesus explained to them that new wine requires new bottles. The old formalities of Judaism cannot contain the new and living way of Christ, his New Covenant.[2] The gospel, though the same "yesterday, today and forever"[3] is at the same time ever new like the life within the seed, ever pregnant and ready to burst forth into new places and cultures.

Could it be that our ineffectiveness in not being a part of the action and growth that should characterize those who handle the 'dynamite' of the gospel is that we try to contain that new wine in outmoded traditions, in obsolete methods, and in habitual forms that may have worked excellently fifty years ago or even today in some other place or circumstance? Because they worked so well for our fathers or grandfathers, we often try to conserve them and force them to carry the new power of the Word in our modern age of technological advancement — and invariably these old wineskins, originally designed to aid the cause of truth, have alas become its obstacles.

The forms are essential to the Word, but if the old wineskins are not discarded they may prevent God's power from flowing in its life-giving stream unto all the world.

What 'traditions' do we have handed down to us in churches of Christ? What are some ways we can up-date our wineskins?

Is Today's Church The Church of the Bible?

When student protesters carry placards that say, "Jesus Yes — The Church No," what are they really saying? Or what is a large percentage of our youth saying who are dropping out and away from the assemblies, young people who avow they believe the Bible and they believe in Jesus as the Christ? Or what is the significance of the figures that show churches of Christ have dropped in thirteen years from number one in church growth to number thirteen now? What is this saying to us? Must we conclude that the greatest roadblocks to our reaching out to the world as well as to our own people already in the fold, somehow must lie within the 'institutions' or 'forms' or 'structures' of our congregations?

The Bible says the church is the body of Christ, the kingdom of God, the bride of Christ, the temple of the Holy Spirit, etc.[4] Christ gave Himself for the church.[5] The church is essential, and those who would dare change the relationship between Christ and the church are accursed for they are tampering with the gospel itself.[6] We cannot please God and glorify Him apart from the church.[7]

The church can present her Lord as Savior and Friend, rather than presenting herself as a program or an institution or a place or a building with which to identify. Too often the church has aligned with traditional denominationalism in its neglect of some weightier matters such as mercy and service shown to the poor, or love demonstrated to the downtrodden man in the inner city, or justice meted out to the person of another race or language or social standing. Has it been too much for us to break out of our walls and go out into the filth and darkness and grime of suffering mankind out there in the streets and alleys? Have we even caught a view of the church as existing outside these walls of comfort?

The time has come for a new idea in the church. We have pushed to its limits the non-biblical concept of building-centered church life. What has been useful in one place or at one time in our history may not apply to the present. A certain nostalgic appreciation for the past is good and necessary for the accurate interpretation of the present. However, we must not allow traditions to continue if they are not continuing to prove themselves beneficial in the present scene. History is a nice place to visit, but we must not live there.

Even a superficial review of our growth patterns shows we are in serious trouble. In a brotherhood that has no headquarters on earth it is not possible to learn exact figures on actual membership at any given time. However from the most reliable sources available,[8] the following growth data emerges:

1940's, 57% increase; 1950's, 171%; 1960's, 17%; 1970's, 6%.

For a radical gospel (the biblical gospel), there must be a radical church (the Bible church). If the message is kept ever-new and fresh, which it must be if it is truly biblical, it must not be limited by obsolete forms or methods.

Some of our most able ministers are predicting vast and sweeping changes will be seen in the churches of Christ in the next few years. They are saying that cataclysmic and drastic advances will be seen as institution-alism and materialism are stripped away. Let us dream a moment as we envision what will be happening when this time comes . . . .

Dream A Moment

First of all, a close examination would be made of the priorities of church buildings and property . . . buildings supposedly purchased during the past twenty years at a greater price than any religious body in history has ever paid! The money could be given to the training and sending of evangelists well-equipped around the world. Store fronts or theatres or halls may be rented for pub-lic assemblies on the Lord's Day. Thought can be given

to discontinuation of Sunday Schools, as parents once again assume the responsibility of teaching their children and the children of their neighbors. Bible studies and prayer meetings in homes take the place of remotely situated midweek services. Spiritual men shepherd these little flocks, sometimes paid but never do they lord it over their charge. All these shepherds in a city know each other well and work together and frequently meet in prayer and in consideration of the spiritual growth and development of their sheep. They intimately know their sheep and their sheep know them. All the neighborhood recognizes their home as a place "where prayer is wont to be made" and where those who assemble there love one another and serve one another and care for one another. By this love, all men know they are disciples of Jesus Christ.[9] Lord's Day memorial celebrations have special meaning to those who have become obedient to the faith and who have been bought with the blood of Christ. Out of a sense of gratitude to their Savior, the disciples serve Him daily by going about teaching and preaching the good news of the kingdom, and exhorting sinners to repent and turn.[10] No consideration is given to economic potential in establishing new churches, but those who give themselves as bondservants to Christ also give as they are prospered with a cheerful heart and thus all their needs are supplied.

It Can Happen Here

And what would happen to such a church? It would grow, and could well re-establish the church described in the book of Acts. In model and in spirit of service to God and man, it would be brought close to the New Testament pattern. Growth would again be described as it was in the first century record: "The Lord added daily," "multiplied," "multiplied greatly," etc. No worries would burden the overseers about building buildings fast enough to accomodate the growing crowds. They would simply rent more or larger halls, and meet in more alone could soar beyond all the combined efforts now seen in the entire brotherhood!

Not New

This concept is not new. In addition to what can be read in the book of Acts, a dozen books could be cited which are written by evangelicals outside our fellowship, all appealing to a return to the simple un-structured, un-political, un-materialistic church described in the New Testament. One prominent author penned these words from a Nazi prison cell some thirty years ago: "The church is the church only when it exists for others. To make a start, it should give away all its property to those in need."[11] Most all these who write come from widely differing theological backgrounds and from far-flung nations of the world. It seems ironic that we who profess to be restoring the New Testament pattern of the church to the world, are not the ones to have introduced and demonstrated these basic principles which are now so universally recognized.[12]

It is no wonder that we are no longer the leader in numerical growth. We have "crossed the tracks" and now are settled down with our successes and blessings and have become fat. It brings to mind what happened to the Israelites. When they had conquered enough land for their own use and sustenance, they stopped fighting. They took their swords and made them into sickles and plows. The valiant fighters from the wilderness became the well-fed farmers of God's promised land that flowed with milk and honey.

And so it has happened to many churches. Their trail-blazing rugged pioneers of faith penetrated the unfamiliar foliage of new territories and cleared new lands, and arose in our grateful minds as heroes in a flame of glory. They delivered to another generation after them many congregations large enough to take care of their own needs, self-sustaining, self-supporting and self-sufficient. The tendency now is to level off and relax from their examples of heroic action on the frontiers, and to take up other tasks related to internal preservation and development.[13]

Here the church has stopped growing. It has failed in developing an expansion of service and concern for the lost soul on the outside. Shall we dare by faith to unlatch the door of unpredictable creativity? Will church leaders be willing to allow new ideas that may jeopardize their absolute control over the church's detailed functions in some areas of human judgment? We believe it must happen, or God may raise up a people somewhere who will fulfill His purposes on this earth in this generation.

Jesus started with twelve men who were determined to cast off the old wineskins (though it proved to be a painful and slow experience), and who were equally determined to retain the pure wine of truth they had received from their Teacher.

> "Give me some men,
> Who are stout-hearted men,
> Who will fight for the right
> They adore;
> Start me with ten
> Who are stout-hearted men,
> And I'll soon give you
> Ten thousand more."[14]

QUESTIONS

1. Give two examples of relative values as taught by Jesus.

2. What is needed for a radical gospel?

3. If Sunday Schools are discontinued, how would our children be taught?

4. Why do you think growth has declined among churches of Christ?

5. Do you believe it is dangerous to dream? Do you agree with the dream expressed in this chapter?

48

FOOTNOTES

1. Luke 5:36-38
2. Hebrews 10:20; Matthew 26:28
3. Hebrews 13:8
4. 1 Peter 5:2; Matthew 16:18; Colossians 1:18; Revelation 21:9
5. Ephesians 5:25
6. Galatians 1:6-9
7. Ephesians 3:21
8. U.S. Census Reports, Statistical Abstract of U.S. Churches, Brotherhood Publishers, Encyclopedias, etc.
9. John 13:34-35
10. Acts 8:4; 3:19; 20:20
11. Bonhoffer, *Letters and Papers From Prison*, The MacMillan Co., N.Y., 1959, 352pp.
12. Two outstanding books from which we have drawn in this chapter are *The Problem of Wineskins*, by Howard A. Snyder, 1VP, 1975, 213pp; and *Disciple*, by Juan Carlos Ortiz, Creation House, 1975, 158pp.
13. For data on church growth patterns see Flavil Yeakley's, *Why Churches Grow*. He projects a cessation of growth in the early eighties. Also see Dewayne Davenport's, *The Bible Says Grow*, and Gerald Paden's *Church Growth* Series in Firm Foundation, beginning February 24, 1981. Paden says, "most congregations in our brotherhood are characterized by non-growth."
14. From the song, "Give Me Some Men," by Oscar Hammerstein and Sigmund Romberg.

Diagrams Of Urban Assembly Patterns   6

The purpose of this chapter will be to portray graphically the assemblies in Jerusalem in the first century and to compare that picture to today's urban assembly pattern among the churches.

There are admittedly some aspects of the Jerusalem church that are not intended to be compared or duplicated in any other place or generation. It had a unique beginning, the presence of apostles, the working of miracles, a community of goods, etc., obviously not intended for all places and all times. But our concern in this study has to do with what made the church grow after the miraculous elements and other unique features were stripped away. How did they attain such great strength and influence so quickly that their enemies acknowledged that "all Jerusalem is filled with this doctrine"[1] and that within a few years tens of thousands had 'flowed into the kingdom' in that city alone?

First we shall view the church in Jerusalem around 50 A.D. The number of disciples is not known, but there were "multitudes," estimated at up to 100,000 souls. We will give special attention to the homes, the temple area, the elders and the treasury.

It is evident that most devotional or worship assemblies (prayers, singing, Lord's Supper, etc.) were conducted in private homes.[2] There were many reasons for this among which would be (1) the newness of the re-

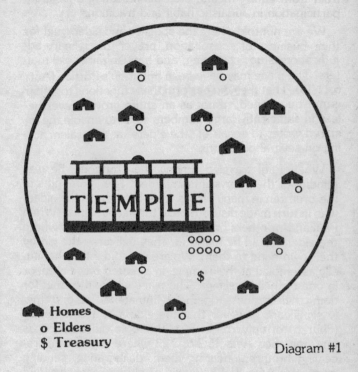

Homes
o **Elders**
$ **Treasury**

Diagram #1

ligion, (2) the poverty of the saints, (3) the persecution by the Jewish leaders, and (4) the convenience and ease of worship at home where the people lived.[3] There were daily gatherings at the Temple area for teaching, fellowship and exchange of news concerning the welfare of the brethren. This may have been the only public gathering place in the city, and a natural place for people to gather whose background was rooted in fleshly and religious Israel. Many Christians, even some of the most respected leaders in the church, continued to maintain their Jewish tribal distinctions, to practice circumcision, refrain from eating meats, etc., all indicating a lingering participation in Judaistic habit and tradition.[4]

We are not told where the apostles and elders met for their business of consultation, prayer, disciplinary adjudication, study, planning, and handling financial matters. The place may have been Solomon's Portico (Acts 5:11-13). That they did perform these functions together is not questioned,[5] if not as an entire group, nevertheless in sufficiently large numbers so as to enable the inspired writer to speak of "the elders" at Jerusalem acting on several occasions.

When Paul traveled among the churches, he was mindful of the poor saints in Judea. The liberal gifts of the brethren in many places were brought to the elders who in turn made distribution to the needy saints.[6] When Paul and/or others brought this relief, they knew where the elders could be found for they delivered the gift by their own hand to them. We are not told if they habitually assembled at the Temple, in a rented office area, or in one of their dwellings. The place where they met for doing their business together is immaterial; it is extremely significant however that the elders of a community (church) of upwards of 50,000 people did function as one unit. See Acts 15:2-6, 2-23 where elders were receiving brethren, hearing them, deliberating, sending men, etc. Acts 21:17-19 tells of elders receiving Paul after his missionary tour.

Can it be reasonably assumed that in most cases where an elder or teacher had particular concern or responsibility, it was a small unit that consisted of a gathering of several families in a residence? Spiritual men like those seven named in the Jerusalem church (chapter 6) could have done teaching and evangelizing even though they may not have been qualified or ordained as elders. Their qualifications are very impressive and their ability to lead an assembly of Christians is obvious: "of good

52

report, full of the Spirit and of wisdom . . . full of faith."[7]
It is not known when elders were ordained in Jerusalem.

Modern Metropolitan Area

The following diagram is an accurate depiction of a city which has members of churches of Christ comparable in numerical strength to that of the Jerusalem church of the first century. Not many cities in America or the world have over 50,000 disciples of Jesus Christ,

Modern Urban Churches

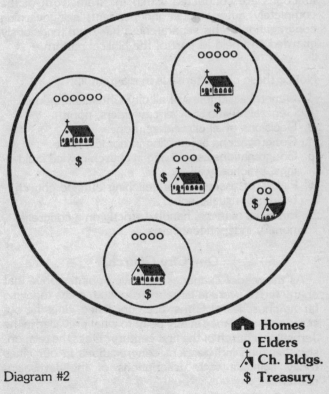

Homes
o Elders
Ch. Bldgs.
$ Treasury

Diagram #2

and perhaps there are none that could count as many as 100,000. The diagram #2 will be accurate in principle wherever there is a multiplicity of congregations.

Wherever churches of Christ exist in urban areas today, the picture will be as shown here (diagram 2). Where there is "fellowship" between these different congregations, there is a doctrinal agreement and sympathetic interest, but the joint participation (fellowship) rarely exemplifies itself. There may be periodic fellowship meals for preachers, or an occasional cooperative evangelistic campaign or teachers' workshop. Beyond these, all functions are conducted within the framework of the completely autonomous, independent, self-governing congregations. This separateness has been tenaciously guarded and held as part of the biblical pattern.

Notice these characteristics in diagram #2:
1. General assemblies of all city Christians, none.
2. General meetings of all city elders, none.
3. Decisions of all city elders, none.
4. Congregations assembling in homes, none.
5. Congregations assembling in church-owned buildings, practically all.
6. Places of assembly for teaching outside church buildings, usually none.
7. Financial matters, handled strictly on a congregationally independent basis.

One City Church?

As the reader examines the seven points above that characterize average large metropolitan areas today so far as churches of Christ are concerned, does he observe a resemblance in any point to what prevailed in the Jerusalem church of the first century? Does the relationship between independent congregations in our cities today coincide with descriptions of the Jerusalem church?

The most striking truth that seems to emerge is that so far as the New Testament record reveals, there was never a plurality of independent congregations within the same city. We frequently read of the church at Corinth, the church at Antioch, the seven churches of Asia (one in each of seven cities), the church in Jerusalem, etc. Whether the city was large or small, does the reader see the Christians there functioning as one church under one eldership? Paul called for the elders of the Ephesus church to meet him at Miletus,[8] which they did. Can you feature a travelling evangelist today calling for the elders of Nashville or Denver or Houston to meet with him as he passed by some thirty miles away? — It would be wonderful to see elders even from a small city or town convene in response to a special call of evangelism. It is most unlikely that any one of even our most highly esteemed brothers could call for and expect a meeting with the elders from a multiplicity of independent congregations within one of our great modern cities.

The editor of the *Millennial Harbinger*[1] spoke in 1849 of the "independence of each Christian community for all its own proceedings," as set forth by the Lord in the 7 letters to the 7 churches of Asia. He reminded his readers that these were "not state or provincial churches but individual communities." He felt there may be "churches of Christ in a city . . . and there may also be but *one* church of Christ in a city or in a province. In both cases a church of Christ is a single society of believing men and women, statedly meeting in one place to worship God." While we would agree with his sentiments properly defined and would honor the opinion of any brother who feels every single regular assembly must constitute the independent church at any "stated" street address, few Bible scholars hold that position especially as it relates to the N.T. urban church setting. How could and why should a huge urban Christian "Community" be bound within the walls of any church house? We believe editor Campbell's concept had been clearly defined earlier when he acknowledged the various house churches or groups in Rome as "one single community"[2] while urging that the "particular congregations" in the different cities were "independent of one another."[11] This is precisely the view we take.

That there is little or no communication, planning, study or prayer among and between elders of different independent modern congregations in the same vicinity is a well known fact. A close relationship is often made impossible by members who move from one church to another. They may have "moved their membership" for any one of several reasons — such as:

1. To find a better teaching program for their children.
2. To worship in a larger congregation.
3. To hear a more powerful, persuasive or pleasing preacher.
4. To avoid impending discipline where their own or their friends' lives are spotted with sin.
5. To escape a financial budget that is not approved by them.
6. To find a more sociable and pleasant atmosphere where doctrinal matters are minimized.
7. To escape the social gospel trend and find a more Bible-centered pulpit and classroom.

Paul stated that the same doctrines are to be taught in every church in every place. The same gospel with a balance of love and kindness and power should be taught in all congregations.[12] Whether we like to admit it or not, there is sometimes a difference from one leadership to another not only in matters of judgment but also in matters of doctrine. Sometimes unqualified men are appointed, resulting in an admitted "wide range of theological difference" within that eldership. It is grievous to the faithful members who hear this, and needless to say, such an eldership will sooner or later create serious confusion within their congregation. When their members seek clarification as to what they believe on basic Bible doctrines, it can be expected they will (1) refuse to give answer and they will (2) refuse to meet with elders or ministers of other nearby congregations in an effort to resolve any problems.

These shameful conditions, when known, make it apparent that the oneness of the Lord's church in that area has been fractured, not only within a congregation but also among the congregations. The church in that city is not "one" in location of assembly nor in doctrinal beliefs. If all the elders in their city had been meeting together as one church, such a breach would have been less likely to occur.

A point often overlooked is that the appointment of a plurality of elders "in every city"[13] seems to have been the same action as appointing elders "in every church."[14] In Crete where Paul left Titus to "ordain elders in every city," there were approximately one million people residing in one hundred cities throughout the 186 mile long island. It is not known how many of these cities had churches. There is no record of *groups* of elders or *groups* of churches within any city in the New Testament record. Jim Kennedy, after returning from a term of preaching in New Guinea, attempted to unite several separate churches in Tullahoma, Tennessee, in 1982 by writing several letters to the elderships. Some churches responded positively, but no significant changes have been made. He made a strong appeal for uniting into one body with one leadership, asking questions such as the following: "When I read the Bible I read about the church at Rome, or Corinth, or Philippi, or Colosse, or Ephesus, or Smyrna, or Thyatira, etc. I *don't* read about the Westside Church, or the First St. Church, or the Hilltop Church that met in these cities. In fact, if Paul were to write a letter to us, who would he address it to? To Wilson Ave.? or Grundy St.? or S. Jackson? Or Westwood or Bel-Aire Dr.? — How would Paul address it to make sure we all read it or had it read to us? — I think he would address it to the "Tullahoma

57

Church." — But what would the Post Office do with such a letter? Who would they give it to? Would we all ever get to hear what it said?"

There was no authority to extend the organization of the church above or beyond the city, so there is no danger of developing an hierarchy or super-organization such as a bishop ovr a plurality of cities.

Walls of Separation?

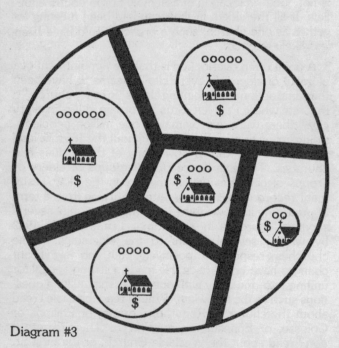

Diagram #3

When several congregations in the same city (or urban area) do not function as one and all the elders meet and work as one, is there a departure from a New Testament pattern? When a weakness develops in the work program or leadership, or a deficiency exists in the physical property where a congregation meets, often this weakness becomes the cause of another congregation's gain. Members sometime remove themselves from the group whose 'program' is lagging or deficient, or whose building may not be as showy and commodious. Elders of congregation "A" which is losing members to congregation "B" are prone to reason, "We are going to have to start a building program if we are going to stay up with congregation "B" which has recently expanded and beautified their facilities." And it isn't long before the members are challenged to give hundreds of thousands of dollars "for Christ" to compete with congregation "B" in the big congregation syndrome. When the addition is made and the financial obligation becomes a reality, the pressure is on all the more to *build up our congregation* even if it is at the expense of losses of our fellow Christians from a nearby assembly. When this unholy spirit prevails, then all kinds of perversions will follow.

How To Pick A Preacher

What may happen in selecting the next preacher? The elders do not feed the flock themselves, so they elect to delegate this important task that God gave them to someone they will hire. The man must be a groomed and polished speaker, a positive thinker who has a record of building up growing congregations where he has been. This decision is a most important one because he will become the principle influence, the chief man in public relations. Surely no one will be chosen who has been chased out of a city for causing a public disturbance through his preaching in the market place, stirred people through his negative approach to the extent that they have literally gnashed at him with their teeth or thrown stones at him in an effort to kill him! And no one whose bodily presence is weak will do the job, even if he is able to write the gospel message effectively. That type of preacher may have worked in the past, even in the first century, but not for us. Not now, anyway. We have a different job in mind and those qualifications are not acceptable. We want growth, but we don't want it to come by unpleasant argumentation with the citizens of the town; that will turn people away and will not build us up. We must have a different type, not too young and not too old, but someone who will be able to attract the youth and comfort the aged.

Where Is The Evangelist's Pulpit?

Now let's back up to basics again. Where does the scripture tell elders to hand their teaching job to someone else? And where is the pattern for an evangelist to do his principle work pastoring in the pulpit of an existing congregation? Are not these some of the traditions

Then

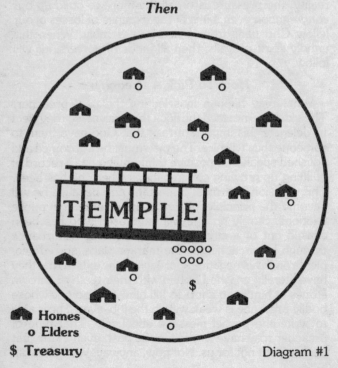

🏠 **Homes**
o **Elders**
$ **Treasury**

Diagram #1

we have developed that need re-evaluation? Remember, brethren, we are obviously doing something wrong. The intention is not to be harsh or unduly critical, but to raise questions about where we can go from where we are to get back to Jerusalem. We cannot do it overnight. Our outmoded traditions will have to be rooted out gradually like the Jewish traditions had to be eliminated over a period of many years in the first century church. Let's first get a good look at the contrast between the Jerusalem church (diagram 1) and the urban churches today (diagram 2).

Now

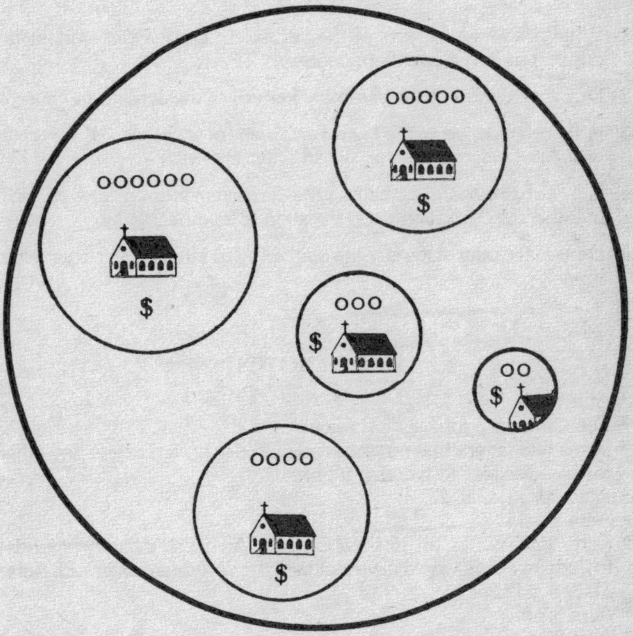

Diagram #2

If we look at the average church of Christ today, we see from 100 to 150 members. They are baptizing 8 each year, including 6 children of their own members. This leaves 2 converts from the outside world. In the process of time, half of these will drop out and taking into account the annual death rate, a net gain of only 1% is realized.

Since the church has no earthly organization or assignment above the level of the church in various city locations, a study of church-building must be at the level of the local congregation. The key to the growth of the universal church is found within the local church, and the key to the growth of the local church is found within the homes of its members to a large extent.

QUESTIONS

1. What are some aspects of the Jerusalem church that cannot be duplicated in the twentieth century?

2. Draw a diagram of the assembly pattern of the Jerusalem church.

3. Is there evidence in the New Testament of a plurality of separate groups of elders within an urban (city) area?

5. Is it probable that members of the Jerusalem church "moved their membership" from one congregation to another? Why?

6. Do you feel any place is more suited to spiritual worship than your home?

FOOTNOTES

1 Acts 5:28
2 See Chapter 3 for full discussion.
3 Jesus had taught that no place is required in preference to any other for His disciples to worship (John 4).
4 Acts 10, 11; Gal. 2.
5 Acts 11, 15.
6 Rom. 15:25-32; 1 Cor. 16:1-3; 2 Cor. 8-9. An earlier delivery of funds to Judean elders would have included the Jerusalem elders. cf. Acts 11:19-30; 12:25.
7 Acts 6:3-5.
8 Acts 20:17
9 Alexander Campbell, *Millennial harbinger*, Bethany, VA, 1849, pages 222-223.

[10] Alexander Campbell, *The Christian System*, Bethany, VA, 1835 p. 76.

[11] Ibid, p. 73.

[12] 1 Cor. 7:17; 16:1-2; Phil. 3:16; Jude 3; 1 Cor. 1:10-13.

[13] Titus 1:5; Phil. 1:1.

[14] Acts 14:23. Also see World Book Encyclopedia and I.S.B.E., article "Crete". When Paul commanded Titus to "appoint elders in every city" he was charging a repetition of what Paul himself had done in Asia when he "appointed elders in every church" (Titus 1:5; Acts 14:23). "A single church seems to have existed in Philippi where there was a plurality of bishops (Phil. 1:1; 4:15)." There was a single church in each city involved where Paul and Barnabas appointed elders. These seem to be the same. (Acts 14:21-23. See Milo Hadwin, *The Role of New Testament Examples as Related to Biblical Authority*, Austin, TX: Firm Foundation, 1974 page 40. See many confirmations of this view in Epilogue.

The
City
Church

7

Urban Church of Tomorrow

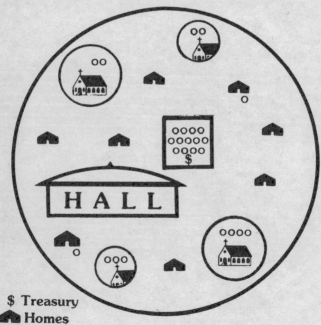

$ Treasury
Homes
o Elders
Ch. Bldgs.

Diagram #4

Here we have a mixture of what we saw in diagrams 1 and 2, in the first century and in the twentieth century. It suggests an integration of the home-congregation with the continued use of church-owned property. If this can be accomplished without black-balling or condemning the brethren who prefer to assemble with small flocks in private residences under the "shepherd-like guidance" of a deacon, pastor, evangelist or teacher, it would seem to be a step in the right direction. We know this simple arrangement appeals to many who profess to believe in God and His Son, Jesus Christ, but who have been repulsed by a long-standing prejudice against the church of Christ. Jesus died for these people the same as for those who have been able to accept our tradition of church houses with their accompanying philosophies of procedure.

A Revealing Survey

In a recent survey taken by evangelists Kelly Lawson and Holland Boring of the Turnpike church in Grand Prairie, Texas (midway between Dallas and Fort Worth), an interesting question was put to thousands of the citizens by means of a telephone machine. The question was not, "Do you go the church somewhere?" That would have turned off most of the people who would have concluded in their hearts, "No, I don't go to church anywhere regularly, therefore I cannot be considered accepted by God." And that would have ended the opportunity to minister to their needs. However, that was *not* the question they asked. Rather, it was, "Do you attend church somewhere, or do you worship God in your home?"

The response to this prudent query was astounding and revealing. Over twenty-five percent (25%) answered they do not attend any church, but that they worship in their home! What does this say to us, if it is not that they believe the Bible (probably an admitted limited knowledge in most cases), but that they are for some reason

65

turned off at the church house. In such cases, shall we write them off as ungodly, without hope and as out of the reach of our ministries? Our soul surely cries out, "NO, we must not leave these souls for whom Jesus died." Ninety percent (90%) of all Americans are totally un-involved in any church relationship.

We must at this point let go of our church building concept and go to them with an alternate biblical pattern of assembly that they can accept and incorporate into their spiritual lives. By sincerely doing this we may be able to reach thousands or even millions to whom we have unconciously been saying, "If you don't come and perform religion our way by our traditional habits and standards, then you can have no part in salvation."

No Leadership

Some small congregations have no elders, hence are handicapped without able leadership. Also, some have only two elders. One may become incapacitated, resign or die, forcing the resignation of the only remaining elder since no church may function biblically without a plurality of overseers. If such assemblies in an urban location were part of an urban church which had multiple places of assembly, the benefits of direction and help would be a definite advantage to this otherwise shepherdless flock. At this point many dwindle and/or die.

A Plea For Vision

We plead with elders of the Lord's church in behalf of this unreached portion of our population, please enlarge your scope of acceptance so as to include those who would worship God in some place on the Lord's Day other than the place we have designated for our convenience. Since Jesus taught us when he spoke to the Samaritan woman at the well, there is no place more sacred than any other surely we cannot say, "This is the place where you ought to worship." That would be no different than to say, "You must worship at this mountain," or "You must go to Jerusalem to be a worshipper of God." Jesus came to abolish this notion that a particular place is more holy than another in true worship to God.

A Church Without Walls

Anyone who reads the New Testament without the colored glasses of his own church's procedures on his nose, will see clearly that a church can function more like a family than like a *company* and that it can grow "without walls." In a book entitled, *Brethren, Hang Loose,* author Bob Girard tells how his Methodist church in Scottsdale, Arizona was organized into small groups for over ten years, then decided to return its church buildings to the denomination and operate in a multiple house-church form.[1] Pastor Girard and his church were expelled from the Western Administrative Area by a formal letter from Virgil A. Mitchell, General Superintendent of the Wesleyan Church, December 20, 1978. Dr. Mitchell quoted the *Discipline* of the denomination reminding that "the Wesleyan church is a denomination consisting of those . . . who hold the faith set forth in The Articles of Religion of the Wesleyan Church . . . who acknowledge the ecclesiastical authority of the Wesleyan Church . . ." The organizational structure was not compatible with that of the denomination's plan of operation.

In a response dated January 8, 1979, Bob Gerard confessed that he and his group "set aside the Discipline" in favor of a "direct response to Scripture." He further wrote, "We cherished the hope that this Word of God would speak more loudly than the voice of the *Discipline* to spiritual men such as yourself."[2]

In such examples from denominational groups' experiences, it is not surprising to see conflicts when the official creeds of their churches are challenged. But for a fellowship such as churches of Christ which has no creed but Christ and no book but the Bible, it should not

67

be expected that fellowship must necessarily be broken over changes in these areas of opinion. The renewal of the simple methods of first century assemblies may be threatening to some because they produce unanticipated problems that need to be worked out, and may put strain on the leaders who will be functioning in circumstances that are unfamiliar to them. But the transition in these areas of judgment could surely be accomplished without notoriety, fanfare or negative reaction.

What Is A City?

A city is "an inhabited place of greater size, population, or importance than a town or village," according to Webster. When we speak of a "metropolitan" or "greater" city, we refer to the principle seat or center of activity encompassing suburban adjacent areas. The word is from the Greek *meter* (mother) + *polis* (city), the mother city. A man may live in a suburban smaller city or town within a greater metropolitan city which is designated by the place of the center of activity (transportation, communication, etc.) Your writer, who lives between Dallas and Fort Worth in Hurst, is sometimes considered a resident of Fort Worth, or even as a resident of the Dallas-Fort Worth Metropolis in some frames of reference. A city like Jerusalem with a wall surrounding it would be more easily defined. The only walled city in North America is Quebec City where the city has spilled over and beyond its walls into what is now greater Quebec City. Smaller suburban towns could be included in the urban church if they so desire, or they may elect to maintain an autonomous church in their own city. An example would be the harbor city of Cenchrea near Corinth, just seven miles away. There was a church at Cenchrea as well as at Corinth (Rom. 16:1). Cenchrea was near, but obviously a separate community from the Corinthian "metropolis". Liberty and charity should govern in all such matters of judgment or opinion.

What Is A Church?

This question is important. To one man "church" or "to go to church" means one thing and to another it may bring to mind something quite different. A small group recently polled came up with these concepts:

1. To go to a building specially designed for worship.
2. To mingle in a social-religious occasion.
3. An assembly of worshippers.
4. A group participating together in a number of different things relating to God and man.

If our group had been larger, more ideas would have been given. A dictionary definition gives the current and popular usages of the word in this order:

"church"

1. a building for public esp. Christian worship.
2. the clergy or officialdom of a religious body
3. a body or organization of religious believers as: a. the whole body of christians, b. denomination, c. congregation
4. public divine worship. (Merriam Webster)

According to the first definition or concept, we would have to conclude that "church" is not even in the Bible! The English language was first spoken on this planet as a Germanic dialect, known as Old English or Anglo-Saxon which began to be spoken in northern England some years after the Anglo-Saxon conquest of that island starting in 449 AD. The earliest written Old English, however, did not appear until approximately 800 AD. If we allow 50 years for the conquest to have its effect on England's native dwellers, that means sometime around 500 AD, the people in northern England started referring to a building erected for worship as a "cirice," later "chirche" and finally "church". Most people do not get the idea at all when they read the word "church" in the Bible. This is a frightening realization. If Jesus died for the church, loved it and shed his blood to purchase it; if it is merely a "building for public worship,"

69

what an unreasonable price He paid!

It would appear to us that translators have a heavy responsibility to give the same words and the same thoughts of the inspired writers of the first century. If they translated the word, a true concept would emerge: the called out, the community, group or company of Christians, the assembly of Christians, the whole body of Christians throughout the earth (Greek-English Lexicon, J.H. Thayer, p. 196).

The church in a city would therefore be the community of believers in Jesus Christ who assemble from time to time at some location(s) within the environs of that metropolis.

In the Old Testament Septuagint, ekklesia has no special religious significance but refers merely to an assembling without defining the nature of the gathering. This could be a mob, or it could be for religious purposes. Philo gave 30 examples of its use and in 25 of these he quotes from the Septuagint (LXX). He does not consider ekklesia as an ecclesiastical word, but a technical term referring to various kinds of assemblies. Cf. Num. 20:10; Ezek. 38:7; Duet. 33:4; Neh. 5:7.[3] This word *ekklesia* is commonly rendered "church" in the New Testament.

In every instance where the church (ekklesia) is referred to in connection with a city, it is in the *singular*. The *plural* form without exception, when referring to location, speaks of a country, a province or a plurality of cities:[4]

churches of Syria	Acts 15:41
churches of Cilicia	Acts 15:41
churches of Asia	1 Cor. 16:19;
	Rev. 1:4, 11, 20; 2:7
churches of Galatia	1 Cor. 16:1
churches of Macedonia	2 Cor. 8:1
churches of cities	Acts 16:4-5
churches of Judea	Gal. 1:22

Putting It All Together

To sum it up, the church, the treasury and elders will be *one* in the urban area. Elders will allow and encourage assemblies anywhere and everywhere that men may gather in the name of Jesus. Congregational autonomy will begin to fade within the city, and individual congregational growth consciousness will give way to the overall growth of the urban church with all its congregations regardless of their place of assembly. An occasional public meeting of all the saints in the city in the largest hall available will afford opportunity for fellowship, encouragement, evangelization and edification.

The people of God can once again fill the great cities with this doctrine and reach such a numerical proportion as to be recognized as the community of Christ in that city to the glory and the praise of Jehovah God.

QUESTIONS

1. Comment on the Lawson-Boring survey.
2. What percentage of Americans are not involved in any church relationship?
3. Define a "city".
4. Define "church".
5. What is the use in the New Testament of the plural term, "churches"?

FOOTNOTES

[1] Robert C. Girard, *Brethren, Hang Loose* (Grand Rapids, MI, 1972). Also see Odin Stenberg's, *A Church Without Walls* (Minneapolis, MN, Bethany Press).
[2] Quoted by L. O. Richards, *A Theology of Church Leadership* (Grand Rapids, MI, Zondervan, 1980), pp. 363-365.

[3] Dr. Jack P. Lewis, QAHAL, Qumran and Ekklesia (unpublished paper), Harding Univ. School of Bible & Religion, Memphis, TN.

[4] The "church" (singular) in the universal sense is often referred to without reference to location (see Matt. 16:18; Col. 1:18). "The church throughout all Judea and Galilee and Samaria" (Acts 9:31), has reference to that portion of the universal church in regions named.

"When Ye Come Together"

8

The expression, "When ye come together," appears four times in the first Corinthian letter (11:18, 20, 33, 34). Similar expressions such as "if the whole church be come together," "when ye are gathered together," "that ye come together," and "ye come not together unto condemnation" are found in 1 Cor. 14:23; 5:4; 11:17,34. In these references we learn that the early church did assemble together.

The question before us in this study is, *"Did the entire church in Corinth meet together every Lord's Day at one place and at one time?"*[1] There is no doubt about the whole church being gathered together upon some occasions such as to hear a notable preacher who was passing through town, to administer a problem of discipline, to receive prophetic exhortations, to pray, or to enjoy a fellowship meal followed by or preceded by the Lord's Supper.

It is improbable that the whole church in Corinth or in any other large city met at one time and place every Lord's Day. It was at that time a church consisting of thousands of Christians in a city of 700,000 population, according to the best information available. There is no evidence that an assembly place would have been available to the disciples for meetings of this magnitude on a regular basis. T.W. Manson says that by 250 AD. there were from thirty to fifty thousand saints in Rome.[2] Chrysostom estimated there were one hundred thousand Christians in Antioch by the fourth century.[3]

The same can be said of the huge church in Jerusalem, with its known membership of 5,000 men plus women and younger people, quickly bringing the number to some 10,000 to 15,000 (see Acts 4:4). Although it cannot be confirmed, some secular historians say the number of disciples may have come to between 50,000 and 100,000 before the dispersion from Jerusalem, and reports of the number of *residents* ranges from 80,000 to 600,000 (as reported in ISBE, Vol. III, p. 1619). Where would this size church meet every Lord's Day with its eldership at any one time and place? Believers were in the Temple every day teaching and praising God, but we have found no scholars who affirm the Temple gatherings to have constituted the orderly and regular Lord's Day worship assemblies including the Lord's Supper, contributions, prayers, singing and preaching. Rather their concensus indicates these regular assemblies of devotion and thanksgiving were in the homes of the saints.

There are numerous acknowledgments in church history, mission reports and biblical exegesis which confirm the position stated above. An example is the following excerpt where Taylor in *Growth of the Church* on pages 224-225 describes a typical Balokoli Anglican fellowship meeting in Uganda Africa: "Their social pattern resembles the household-clusters of the first generation of the church, gathered on the estate of a landowner . . . Their rallying point is the fellowship meeting, usually held at some time on Sunday, and on one other evening of the week." Gailyn Van Rheenan notes how the church of Christ in Uganda was forceably closed by soldiers and the Christians were beaten July 2, 1973. After this time, Christians in western Uganda have continued to meet secretly and leaders have experienced severe persecution.[4]   In all similar circumstances of persecution from the beginning of the church, homes have been the principle place of assembling.

There are some who contend that for a church to be a church, fully organized with elders and deacons, it must assemble each Lord's Day *all together at one time and at one place;* and that only this way can the elders "oversee" and watch the flock. This we believe to be an erroneous assumption, incapable of verification either from the divine or secular accounts of the New Testament church. This extreme position would require that a building be purchased or acquired every Lord's Day on a regular basis that is large enough to get the whole church seated at the same time. How could this be in Jerusalem or at any other city where the church had grown to number 20,000 to 50,000 souls? We have some American cities with this many disciples. The reader might bear in mind also that there was never a plurality of separate and autonomous "churches" within any city so far as the New Testament record reveals. Some feel that Rome may be an exception. It becomes evident in view of these observations that the city church had multiple places of assembly.

If it be contended that a church may not congregate except it be all at one time and in one place, then several practical problems arise in the modern church. The first we have already mentioned, and that is:

(1) Church properties would have to be expanded to meet the growth, particularly the main auditorium or assembly auditorium. The church could not grow beyond its ability to purchase larger and larger facilities.

(2) A church could not assemble in "early" and "late" services, even if part of the elders met with each assembly.

(3) The church could not include other language segments, such as Spanish or German, unless they met at the same time and place and used an interpreter (or re-

mained ignorant and unable to participate).

(4) Deaf persons would be eliminated for the same reasons as (3) above.

(5) There could be no worship assembly with the sick or aged who are unable to attend where the whole church comes together.

(6) There could be no gatherings in homes when circumstances of weather conditions or lack of available transportation prevented traveling to the "one place" of assembly.

(7) The Lord's Supper could not be served to a portion of the saints on Sunday evening.

The elders of the Midtown church wrote in defense of their separate groups assembling to accomodate the peculiar needs of various languages and functions: "In looking at Hebrews 10:25, it is a mistake to assume that this Scripture's intent is to bind us to a one room general assembly, all other arrangements being wrong. For example, few would argue that the Laotians or bus ministry workers got up on Sunday morning, came to the building to assemble together to sustain the gospel on earth, are really forsaking to assembly together since they are in another room. They are very much with us in sustaining the Lord's work in this local congregation. A Spanish assembly also has been started; meeting in a separate place, yet functioning as a part of this great church under the same overseers. Sunday evening assemblies accomodate those with shift-work commitments and for adult teachers who care for children in Sunday morning's Children's Training for Worship Program."[5]

Not only *may* the above cited liberties be exercised in our assembly patterns, but they *must* be if we would be flexible, charitable and practical in these areas of human expediency and opinion. If we could be transported in time back to the first century church at Corinth or Jerusalem, do you suppose we could find a 1,000 member church meeting at Fourth and Elm, at Tenth and Broadway, at 5800 Nazareth Road, or at Fifth and Lowland Streets? It is certain we would find no church buildings, and almost as certain that we would have to know the names of some disciples in whose homes several of the saints would be meeting for worship. One home may have thirty gathering with an able and trusted teacher; another may be meeting in the home of an elder with twenty. We may learn where Macedonians or Romans are gathering, or another place where the deaf render praise. Occasionally these groups would all be drawn together to hear Paul preach when he returns from a preaching tour, or to enjoy a love feast and worship period in a huge public building or open place. And of course the elders would all work together in their oversight of the church in that city.

"The challenges and opportunities of the big city are as multitudinous and variegated as the individuals living in it," says Ron Prater of Sao Paulo, Brazil.[6] He lists some distinct challenges peculiar to the giant urban communities which can best be overcome in the manner of church plantings described in the New Testament. (1) The population itself is a challenge, as in his city there are some ten million souls. (2) The distances involved in getting about within the megalopolis could be as much as 3 or 4 hours. Bus travel is slow, traffic jams are serpentine, many streets are new and unregistered on city maps, many do not have telephones and the expense and time in attending assemblies far away may dishearten members, especially in the evenings. (3) Real estate in the big city is more expensive and obtaining church property is financially oppresive. It is our firm conviction that the problems faced can be solved best with work and sacrifice through the power of God working in us (Eph. 3:20), by one church in the city meeting in numerous house groups under one leadership, as was evidently the case in the first century. And how glorious it would be upon occasion for the whole church to all meet together in some big arena for a celebration of praise and triumph!

Let us try to remove our 20th Century religious colored glasses so that we might catch a fresh, clear view of the simple beauty of the assemblies of first century Christians.

QUESTIONS

1. Did the entire church come together on some occasions at Corinth?

2. The disciples in what city met together in a large upper room "to break bread" and also to hear a notable travelling evangelist?

3. Is there evidence that the whole church in Jerusalem met each week at one time and place in a concerted, orderly assembly?

4. Name some practical problems that arise if the entire church must meet at the same time and place each Sunday.

5. Did the church at Corinth have elders?

FOOTNOTES

[1] J.H. of Virginia writes: "It is *certain* that we must meet as a whole church every Sunday for the Lord's Supper." (Letter, May 15, 1981). This view, though expressive of an ideal, we do not hold to be an absolute obligation as this chapter explains. Hardeman Nichols in an open forum at the Fort Worth Lectures, January, 1982, said the "whole church" meeting together represents an "ideal" but that Paul knew exceptions would occur such as the sick, travelers, etc. See Epilogue for fuller report.

[2] T.W. Manson, *The Church's Ministry*, London: Hodder & Stoughton Ltd., p. 70.

[3] Waymon Miller, *New Testament Churches*, Tulsa: Plaza Press, page 25.

[4] Gailyn Van Reenan, Church Planting in Uganda, 1976, Wm. Carey Library, Pasadena, CA., pages 35, 65-66.

[5] Midtown Elders, July 9, 1980 (published letter, Ft. Worth, Texas).

[6] Ron Prater, Firm Foundation, p. 534, August 25, 1981.

The Church That Is In Their House

9

R eference has been made in chapter two to the Jerusalem church and its gatherings for devotion and praise "from house to house." This chapter will deal with other New Testament references to saints who met in homes in other cities.

Priscilla And Aquila

Priscilla and Aquila were expelled as Jews by an edict from Rome and were first found at Ephesus. They later returned to Rome. The "church that is in their house" is spoken of at both places (Romans 16:3-5; 1 Corintians 16:19; Acts 18:2,26), rendered as "congregation", "group", "community", or simply "those who meet" in various translations. Albert Barnes comments on Romans 16:5: " 'The church that is in their house.' This may mean either the church that was accustomed to assemble for worship at their hospitable mansion; or it may mean their own family with their guests, regarded as a church. In those times Christians had no houses erected for public worship, and were therefore compelled to meet in their private dwellings."[1] In their home, a group of Christians met to worship. Would this not be the answer to the problem of moving into a community where there is no church? Start one in your home. Moses E. Lard wrote in 1875:

"In that early day, the disciples were without meeting houses. The private houses of brethren were the only places open to them. And from no hearts on this earth, I venture to think, has purer or more acceptable worship ever ascended to God than from these unworldly little groups. More of art and splendour can certainly be found in great fanes erected to God; but from these great houses, with their gorgeously appareled crowds, He often delights to turn away, I doubt not, as from a sham, and find a delightful seat amidst the 'poor in spirit' who make the 'church in their house.' The lowly Master . . . without a place 'to lay his head,' presents a humiliating contrast to many of the 'churches' of the present day, piled up in gratification of folly, and with no notice from him, 'dedicated' to his name."[2]

"It seems then," reflects Matthew Henry, "a church in a house is no such absurd thing as some make it to be. Perhaps there was a congregation of Christians that used to meet at their house at stated times . . . others think that the church was no more than a religious, pious, well-governed family that kept up the worship of God. Religion and the power of it, reigning in a family, will turn a house into a church . . . When Priscilla and Aquila were at Ephesus, though but sojourners there, yet there also they had a church in their house (1 Cor. 16:19). A truly godly man will be careful to take religion along with him wherever he goes."[3]

Rome, Ephesus, Colossae

In greeting Philologus, Julia, Nereus and Olympus at Rome by name, Paul also greets "all God's people associated with them" (Rom. 16:15 NEB). Nymphas was associated with a church (congregation) in his house in the city of Colossae (Col. 4:15), and Philemon met in his own house in the same city with Apphia and Archippus in "the church" (Philemon 2). While there are problems related to 'house churches,' there are at the same time many distinct benefits associated with such an arrangement. Dr. Jerry Jones elaborated upon seventeen

80

advantages of house churches in a lecture in Boston where twenty-six such groups comprise the church there (see chapter on Boston for more information on the development and success of this work).[4]

We have observed that in Rome, Ephesus and Colossae, the church consisted of several groups that assembled in private houses of the brethren. The church in each city was addressed by Paul as though all the saints as one body at each place should receive his letter. No evidence has been available that would prove separate congregational autonomy existed within any of these cities, or in any city, in the early church of Jesus Christ, despite the fact that there were multiple places of assembly. When Paul wrote "to the saints" at Rome, Colossae or Ephesus, he was writing collectively to the church in each city the same as when he addressed "the church" at Corinth and Thessalonica.

The Angel Of The Church

When we view the church in each city as above outlined, the need for an "angel" of the church becomes evident. The Greek term "angelos" simply means a messenger. Jesus spoke to John on Patmos about an "angel" in each of the seven churches in the seven cities addressed in Revelation chapters one, two and three. Their assignment was to see that every member of the Christian community in each of their respective cities received the spiritual messages from the Lord.

Knowing it would be hard if not impossible to ever get all His church together at one time and place in any given city, the Lord told John to send out seven special letters into the care of trusted messengers called "angels". There was an angel at the church in each of these cities: one at Ephesus, at Smyrna, at Pergamum, at Thyatira, at Sardis, at Philadelphia, and one at Laodicea. In this way, the Lord had assurance that His word would get to every Christian in every one of the seven cities. They could not just call everybody together at the church house, because there weren't any. And if there had been, if it was then like it is today in the church, some of the members would have been away on vacation or fishing or working or sick — or just plain unresponsive to the call to assemble.

It is a matter of biblical and historical significance that the church in each city in these first centuries customarily assembled in several homes of its members. One letter was addressed to "all the saints" in the city of Rome, though they regularly worshipped in at least half a dozen houses or groups (Rom. 16). Have you ever wondered who would have received such a letter, accepting the responsibility to see to it that all in the church could read it? It must have been someone known to be committed to the task of delivering communications to every saint. With this in mind we can appreciate more the responsibility that was placed upon the "angel", God's special messenger for the local church.

The Upper Chamber

The gathering together at Troas (Acts 20:4-12) was a special meeting to welcome and to hear the apostle Paul with his eight travelling companions. They waited for seven days for the regular Lord's Day meeting when the Lord's Supper was observed. Paul preached to a large gathering in a third story "upper-chamber" where there "were many lights" (verse 8). We are not given further information on this place of assembly, but can only conclude that it was either (1) a large rented hall, (2) a large upper room in a private dwelling loaned for the occasion, or else (3 a meeting hall owned by the church. One of the first two options is more probably the case: a hired or leased space for the special gathering of the local and visiting brethren to use for this memorable occasion, or a large private dwelling.

In 1974-75 Ralph Arceneaux did research in the graduate school of business administration at Midwestern State University. In this study entitled "Empty Cathedrals" he reported church facilities (auditoriums, edu cational buildings and parking lots) are used less than 2% of the time based on a ten-hour day and seven-day week. His survey further revealed a total asset value of $35,000,000 among 100 churches reviewed in one city, which he then contrasted with a major industrial plant in the same community which had a comparably valued physical plant. Arceneaux observed, "It would be sheer folly to expect that corporation (Pittsburgh Plate Glass Corporation) to operate that facility one day a week and only an hour or two of that day." Further research in 1979 sought for explanations of the extra-ordinarily low utilization of religious facilities . . . concluding that "the church has drifted into idolatry in erecting vast church structures that dominate the budgets of many congregations, and for some the major item over the entire history of the congregation has been for real estate, buildings and general operating expenses."[5]

Because of the silence of scripture with reference to the ownership or arrangements of buildings in which they met, no laws or regulations concerning such should be made today. This writer is not questioning, therefore, the *right* of a church to own a building, to rent a building, or to borrow a building for a place to assemble. Whatever is wise and appropriate for the occasion at hand and that will not hinder or prevent any other obligations, would most certainly be acceptable to God.

The Household of God

Within the church today there is a mass of people who believe that success with God is to be measured by becoming and being something better in the *inner* man. With them, success on either the personal or congregational level is not measured by a proliferation of building programs, crusades, seminars, filmstrips and all the other paraphernalia that meets the public eye. They see, rather, in the New Testament many references to the "household" as a basic social *and religious* unit, a more close and intimate level of relationship than can be offered by larger structures.

Paul became a part of a household while on his preaching tours. In Corinth he became a member of the household of Aquila and Priscilla. Then, he continued next door to the synagogue in the house of Titus Justus (Acts 18:1-8). A similar pattern is followed in Thessalonica involving the house of Jason who incurred legal responsibility for the conduct of the disciples (Acts 17:1-9). Paul referred to his preaching "from house to house" as well as publicly (Acts 20:20), indicating not only the location of the proclamation, but also that the message was directed to the household and sometimes converts were made of entire households (Acts 11:1-14; 16:15,31-34; 18:8; 1 Cor. 1:14-16). It must not be overlooked that Christian communities come into existence in this manner.

After Cornelius and his household heard Peter in his house (even though by custom he could have no contact with a Jew), he and all his household were baptized. They then took Peter and his companions into his household (Acts 10:47f) where his generous hospitality became known to the Jews in Jerusalem (Acts 11:3). Lydia is another similar case: when she was baptized, she prevailed upon Paul to "come to my house and stay" (Acts 16:15).

Units of Churches

It was normal for the church in any particular city to be made up of one congregation meeting in a home. However, as time progressed, this would not continue. The spread of the message by implanting the seed in many sectors of the city would give rise to the formation of other groups. We know that in some cities there were a number of house churches. When Paul wrote in 1 Thessalonians 5:27, he urged that the letter be read "to all the brethren," suggesting the existence of more than one assembly in Thessalonica. Even if the Bible had not explicitly mentioned a plurality of household churches in a city, it would not be unreasonable to assume that

a number of such groups would exist there after pro-
longed evangelistic activity. This has happened in our
own generation as well. For example, there is the case
of Vijayawada, India, where preaching in various sectors
of that populous city gave rise to some fifty household
churches, each blossoming where the seed had been
sown.

The information on the organizational relationship
between these house churches in the New Testament
has not been sufficiently recognized by students of the
early Christian community. The leaders of the church
in Jerusalem had responsibility for the whole church
there. The same was true in Crete where elders were
appointed in every city (Titus 1:5). Paul and Barnabas
appointed elders in every church they had established
(Acts 14:23). These churches were still small enough
to meet in one household per city, so that the church
in that city would be identical with one household; or
the writer may have been thinking of the church in each
city as being made up of all the household assemblies
in that town.

In the context of these truths, statements dealing with
the leaders' qualifications can better be understood.
For example, elders must be hospitable and deacons
must manage their households well if they would be-
have properly "in the household of God" (1 Timothy
3:2-4, 12-15).

China

"One of the most exciting developments in twentieth-
century church history is taking place today in China,"
writes Jonathan Chao in 1982.[6] He says they closely
resemble the "diffuse" New Testament church in the
way they have survived, even thrived, in adverse po-
litical climate . . . increasing by the thousands in house
churches. Although it is impossible to obtain precise
statistics for China as a whole, China Church Research
Center's staff and friends estimate there are between
25 and 50 million believers in house churches. The

movement is not of recent origin, but is an extension of independent groups that began in 1911 and a similar indigenous movement that grew out of persecutions in the twenties, all free of foreign missionary control. Even before the Communist revolution in 1949, hundreds of thousands of Chinese Christians were associated with several thousand house meetings. Practically all of these began from small prayer meetings that developed into regular worship assemblies then evangelism and some type of organization followed in some instances.

We've Come A Long Way!

We got where we are with our heavy over-burden of church real estate by a process of evolution from very small beginnings. Many of us can remember when the church met in a small frame building or in a home. Our mothers baked the communion loaf and laundered the cloth that covered it; our dads taught the classes and 'brought the lesson' when it came their turn.

In contrast to those humble days (when we were growing numerically at a greater rate percentage-wise than at any time since the first century), we now have hundreds of the finest, most expensive church-owned buildings that can be found. It is not uncommon to hear of multi-million dollar building programs. One church has a 15-year bond retirement obligation that involves repayment in principle and interest of $571,000 during one year alone. One Texas congregation in one day in 1984 raised over $8,000,000 in a building fund campaign planned by a professional fund raising company. We have apparently reached a portion now that no one person or even one generation had planned or intended. To turn the trend when we are so untrained in home-church experiences may prove to be a difficult and delicate procedure. Some predict it will take 25 years, others say 300 years, and yet others say the trend cannot be reversed short of a miracle of God or to go to another city where there is no existing church.

QUESTIONS

1. Name a Christian couple who had a church in their house. What city?

2. What procedure is suggested here for beginning a church upon moving to a city?

3. Who is quoted in this chapter concerning "great houses erected to God" with "their gorgeously appareled crowds"?

4. Comment on Jesus having no place to lay His head, in the light of the ornate edifices erected for Him today.

5. What experience or training is necessary to conduct home-worship today?

6. To what dangers or abuses are home-churches liable? How can they be prevented?

FOOTNOTES

[1] Albert Barnes Commentary on Romans (Comments on 16:5).

[2] Commentary on Romans by Moses E. Lard, pp 454f.

[3] Matthew Henry's Commentary, Vol. 6, p. 478.

[4] Dr. Jerry Jones, "House Church". Tape recorded lecture, World Evangelism Seminar, October, 1984. A series of studies was written by him later. Contact the publisher for information on their availability.

[5] Ralph Arceneaux, Firm Foundation, Austin, TX: Nov. 2, 1982, p 699.

[6] Christianity Today, June 18, 1982, pp 24-26.

Hospitality
An Expression
Of Love

10

A rather extensive search by religious sociologists has been made in an effort to determine the nature of the relationships that existed between early Christians: their home life, their community life, and the social structures of their assemblies.[1]

The practice of hospitality (Gk., philozenos, lover of strangers) was urged upon the disciples in such passages as Romans 12:13, 1 Timothy 3:2, Titus 1:8, 1 Peter 4:9, Hebrews 13:1-2 and Matthew 25:34-43:

"Share with God's people who are in need; practice hospitality" (NIV, Rom. 12:13).
". . . love people enough to invite them into his home" (1 Tim. 3:2; Titus 1:8, SEB).
"Invite one another into your homes without complaining about it" (1 Peter 4:9, SEB).
"Don't forget to welcome strangers into your home" (Heb. 13:1-2, SEB).
"I was a stranger and you took me into your home" (Matt. 25:35, SEB).

The main subject of 3rd John is the extension of hospitality to fellow Christians. Like our own society, the Romans of the first century were highly mobil. Paul established churches along the main trade routes and like himself, many of his converts were transients. When you read his letters, you will be impressed with the mobility of his co-workers also. Christian travelers would prefer to avail themselves of their brothers' hospitality.[2]

The opening of the disciples' homes to strangers was further manifested because the religious services seem to have been conducted primarily in hospitable homes. Paul, on some occasions, converted entire households and he then used them as bases for his operations in evangelizing.[3] The "host" or Christian "patron" in whose house the church met was also open for traveling Christians in at least two instances.[4] Phoebe is described in Romans 16:2 as "prostatis," that is evidently a "patronness" or representative, perhaps even a bonded legal representative of the Cenchrea church, much like Jason in Thessalonica. The description implies that she hosted a church in her house as he did. Since Paul's writings did not accord authority to women in the church (1 Cor. 14:33-37), it is clear that her role as "patronness" of the church acknowledged her as a hostess and servant rather than as an authoritative office holder. The qualifications of both elders and deacons, however, did include descriptions of their behavior in their own households (1 Tim. 3:4ff; 3:12; 5:4).

When we consider the bishop as a man who knows how to take care of his own household and as one who is to be hospitable, some may assume that he had a church in his own home and that he ruled over it. But there is nothing in the Bible to force the concept that he derived his authority as an elder (bishop) merely on the basis that the church met in his house, or on the basis that he was hospitable. All Christians were exhorted to be hospitable. Furthermore, the rule or authority of the elders was always spoken of as in the *plural* with relation to the church or the flock within their city. If a group of Christians congregated in his home, obviously he would develop a special and intimate relationship with that particular group, but his "official" supervision or rule would be in conjunction with all the bishops in the church of his city.[5]

The information on the relationship between these small house groups in the city is very limited, but we do have some insights into Rome, Colossae, Thessalonica and Laodicea. These groups were separate within each locality and yet they were united in such a way that one letter was sufficient for the angel (messenger) to reach all the groups. Although there was a multiplicity of groups of disciples in a particular locality, they were not isolated or "autonomous", but thought of themselves as together comprising the body, the church, the community of Christ in that locality.[6]

Gaius and Diotrophes

As we now look again to 3rd John, perhaps a clearer idea emerges because we have this background information in mind. Here we have a letter written concerning some traveling brethren who had met with mixed receptions by people addressed in the same letter. Gaius, on the one hand, received the travelers warmly and then sent them away on their journey (verses 5-8). However, Diotrophes rejected both the former letter and those who carried it (verses 9 and 10). What about the relationship between Gaius and Diotrophes? They evidently each had gathered a circle of friends (philoi), and Diotrophes seems to have exercised some control over his group. Gaius does not seem to be a part of Diotrophes' group, but there is no record of any conflict between the two of them.

Diotrophes' action is not receiving the brothers and then stopping those who want to welcome them and throwing them out of the church (ektes ekklesias ekballei, verse 10), has been pictured by some scholars as an "excommunication" by Bishop Diotrophes! This is an unwarranted conclusion, as nothing is said in the text about Diotrophes holding any kind of office in the church. He did love to be "first" or "pre-eminent", but his *power* in our judgment did not rest on *ecclesiastical* authority. It is rather a lack of hospitality that John is reproving. Diotrophes had refused to extend hospitality any longer to any members who opposed him. Neither Gaius nor Diotrophes "held any office" or authority by virtue of their hospitality. However, Diotrophes did have the power to reject anyone who opposed him from assembling in his house.

[This discussion has been extended beyond what I had originally attempted in my first writing. I feel obligated to clarify my position on the relationship between an elder and the group that assembles in his house, since it has been misconstrued.]

QUESTIONS

1. Describe the role of "host" of a church.

2. What role do you see Phoebe filling in the Cenchrea church?

3. Was Diotrophes a bishop? Where did he get his power to put people out of the church?

4. Were Gaius and Diotrophes at odds with each other?

5. Should one elder "rule over" the group of Christians that assembles in his home?

6. Although Paul had never been in Rome, how many personal acquaintances live there whose name he calls? How many groups or "house churches" made up the community of disciples at Rome?

FOOTNOTES

[1] See a sketch of a few of these works in Epilogue, section "New Material." Of special help has been the work of Dr. Abraham Malherbe, Professor of N.T. Criticism and Interpretation, Yale Divinity School. His chapters on House Churches and Hospitality are particularly beneficial.

[2] Acts 21:4,7,16f; Rom. 15:28f; 16:1f; 1 Cor. 16:10f; Phil. 2:29; Philemon 22; Rom. 12:13; Heb. 13:2.

[3] Acts 18:1-8; 17:6f; 16:15, 31ff; 1 Cor. 1:14-16; 16:19 etc.

[4] Rom. 16:13; Philemon 2, 22.

[5] See the plurality of elders in each church (city) in Titus 1:5; Acts 20:28; Acts 14:23. These documents and letters describe presbyters (bishops, elders) with respect to cities, not individual groups within the city.

[6] Abraham Malherbe, Social Aspects of Early Christianity, p. 101. Fortress Press, Philadelphia, 1983.

Shepherds Of The Sheep

11

"And the word of Jehovah came unto me, saying, Son of man, prophesy against the shepherds of Israel, prophesy, and say unto them, even to the shepherds, Thus saith the Lord Jehovah: Woe unto the shepherds of Israel that do feed themselves! should not the shepherds feed the sheep? Ye eat the fat, and ye clothe you with the wool, ye kill the fatlings; but ye feed not the sheep. The diseased have ye not strengthened, neither have ye healed that which was sick, neither have ye bound up that which was broken, neither have ye brought back that which was driven away, neither have ye sought that which was lost; but with force and with rigor have ye ruled over them. And they were scattered, because there was no shepherd; and they became food to all the beasts of the field, and were scattered. My sheep wandered through all the mountains and upon every high hill: yea, my sheep were scattered upon all the face of the earth; and there was none that did search or seek after them. Therefore, ye shepherds, hear the word of Jehovah:

Ezekiel 34:1-7

There are three words in the Greek New Testament that are used to apply to the work of the shepherd of God's people. They are *episkopos* (translated bishop and overseer), *poimen* (shepherd, pastor), and *presbuteros* (presbyter, elder).[1] Although our common versions do not translate *poimen* as "shepherd," the idea this word brings in the Greek language (as in Ephesians 4:11) is at the heart of what an elder should be and do.

With The Sheep

The shepherd must be "with" or "among" or "in the

midst of" the flock.[2] This cannot be done by pronouncement and announcement. The shepherd does not lead the sheep by shouting and commanding from a distance, "Okay, you over on the south slope, get on!" He must be accessible. Jesus, the Chief Shepherd, was and is always available. Any man or group of men that cannot be approached except through fifteen yards of red tape is not a shepherd of the sheep. He may be a good business director, an astute financial manager, or even have an excellent knowledge of the Bible, but he is not a shepherd of the sheep.

Training The Sheep

There is only one reason that the scripture requires that an elder be "apt to teach"[3] and that is so he can teach. He must feed the flock [4] and train them. Evangelists and teachers may instruct, "reprove, rebuke and exhort" (2 Tim. 4:2), but the elders are to feed, nurture and train.

The Bible always speaks of a plurality of elders who feed the flock, the local church body (Acts 20:28). Some have erroneously assumed that all the church is required to meet at one time and place where and when the elders are to feed them as "the flock." When we consider Peter's relationship to "the flock" in Jerusalem, it is evident that the above cannot be held as obligatory or even possible! Peter, an elder (1 Peter 5:1-2) in Jerusalem, exhorted elders everywhere to "tend the flock of God which is among you." How could Peter get all "the flock" of 50,000 sheep, more or less, together in Jerusalem at one time and place to feed them and tend them on a regular daily or weekly basis? Obviously he worked in conjunction with all the overseers, but he personally had a particular care and concern for the smaller group whom he knew more intimately, meeting daily and/or each Lord's Day in a private dwelling.

A Worthy Example

They must be above reproach, respectable, devout

men, worthy of double honor,[5] to be looked to and followed. Paul said to mark him as like Christ, and to imitate him to the extent that they saw Christ in him.[6] The Christ in the Book is best seen in the Christ of the Look! We can best see Him when seen in the lives of His disciples . . . "Christ in you is the hope of glory!"[7]

Men of Vision

Where there is no planning, no forward look, the people will perish. "Be it unto you according to your faith."[8] Paul writes, "Now unto him that is able to do exceedingly abundantly above all that we ask or think, according to the power that worketh in us, unto him be the glory . . ." There is no end to what a congregation can attain with this kind of faith.

Stable Family Unit

Children and wife see in the father a leader worthy of emulation in spiritual matters. He is heard in prayer often in the home, and seen and heard in reading the Word of God. He is seen weeping over the story of Christ, and his sternness is observed with set of jaw as error is confronted. His children see his smile and joy when a sheep returns to the fold, or when a new birth adds a lamb to the flock.

Restorers Of The Wayward

The good shepherd protects his flock against dangers, and every sheep against straying. Bringing them back through caring correction is a mark of love and concern.[9] Discipline is unheard of in some congregations because shepherds don't know their sheep and they don't care when they wander off and perish. The hireling may say, "How can we withdraw from him when he has already withdrawn from us?" The Bible says there are only two ways out of the earthly body of Christ: (1) to die and go to heaven[10] and (2) to be withdrawn from.[11] Until then every member should be cared for by a shep-

94

herd or a leader somewhere. The wayward, the fallen and the weak are objects of the elder's special prayer and concern. This begins at the first signs of sickness, and must not be neglected until an autopsy on a dead spiritual corpse is performed to see what caused the death.

Life And Faith

The faith of the shepherd is to be imitated and the issue of his life is to be observed.[12] Men of faith can do beyond their ability,[13] because God works through men of faith and commitment. Faith comes by hearing God's message.[14] That is why the elder is diligent in hours of prayer and study of the Bible. Even when his car rolls, so does his tape recorder also roll! Yes, he has some good cassette tapes and hears men of faith inspire and instruct when he is driving.[15] The word of God dwells in him richly in all wisdom![16]

Concern For Other Sheep

The shepherd is concerned about the sheep in his fold, in his pen. But Jesus has *other* sheep that *must* be brought into the fold.[17] Bring them in from the fields of sin, bring the little ones to Jesus. God holds the elder responsible for watching the sheep, and he shall give account.[18] He also seeks others to feed.

Get The Picture

After reading the above, does the shepherd-sheep relationship sound more to you like one man working with twenty or thirty souls, or like a group of four or five men collectively working as a kind of board of directors supervising five hundred or a thousand souls? Which picture do you get from John 10:1-17? Which picture do you get from Ezekiel chapter 34? Please read these two passages carefully together with the description of the great church in Jerusalem with its many household assemblies.

QUESTIONS

1. What are the six English words applied to the office or work of Shepherd of the church?

2. Comment on Hebrews 13:7. Name two areas vital to the life of a shepherd.

3. Can you describe the "power that worketh in us" (Eph. 3:20)?

4. Does the Shepherd have responsibilities toward sheep that are not of his own fold?

5. What value can a cassette tape recorder be to an elder of the church?

6. Discuss the eldership as a "board of decision-makers and financial managers."

7. Have we restored the church of the New Testament?

FOOTNOTES

[1] Acts 11:30; 15:2; 1 Tim. 5:17; Titus 1:5; 1 Tim. 3:1-7; Eph. 4:11.
[2] 1 Peter 5:2
[3] 1 Tim. 3:2 [Also see Charles Hodge, *My Elders*, Star Bible, Fort Worth, 1976), pages 45-57 on "Qualifications of Elders."]
[4] Acts 20:28
[5] 1 Tim. 3:1; 5:17; Titus 1:8
[6] 1 Cor. 11:1
[7] Col. 1:27
[8] Eph. 3:20-21
[9] Heb. 12:3-13
[10] Rev. 2:10
[11] 2 Thess. 3:6
[12] Heb. 13:7
[13] 2 Cor. 8:3
[14] Rom. 10:17
[15] A sterling example would be a cassette tape by Reuel Lemmons entitled, "The Chief Shepherd Was With The Sheep," Sunset's Fifth Annual Elders' Workshop, 1980. This is a classic description of sheep and shepherd.
[16] Col. 3:16
[17] John 10:16 [This refers specifically to Gentiles who would later be included as Jesus' disciples. The principle is in harmony with the last charge given in Mt. 28:18-20 to "teach all men" throughout the world.]
[18] Heb. 13:17

[For much of the information in this chapter we gratefully acknowledge a cassette recording of Richard Rogers' recap of the 1980 elders workshop at Sunset.]

A Church Brand — To Wear Or Not To Wear

12

What name should the church use if it is to be most beneficial in aiding the rapid growth of Christianity in the city? How was the first century church identified?

A Mark

The most obvious mark of a denomination is the taking and wearing of a distinctive name. That name could be either a biblical name or an unbiblical name. Whether it be "Church of God" (which several distinct denominations have chosen as "their" name) or "Baptist Church" (which even more groups have selected), each has adopted and agreed to wear that distinctive name. Thus, when a person hears the name, he is able to identify the group, its doctrine, organization, history, liturgy, etc., and tuck it away into its proper place.

It has been our observation during the past few years that the average member of the entire religious community is unhappy and discouraged with denominational division. Even the most devout supporters of these church groups are becoming more reluctant to say, "I am a Methodist", or "I am a Baptist". Often we hear, "I am a Christian first, and a _____ second." Very few if any of the faithful members of these churches whom

97

we have met take issue with the concept of being a "Christian only," simply a member of the body of Christ.

When Paul warned against taking distinctive party names in the church at Corinth, was the group identified as "Christ" Christians any less of a faction than the other divisions that denominated themselves by other names? The point is this, that a man or a group may denominate themselves with a biblical or an unbiblical name, and in either case be prompted by an exclusive or sectarian spirit.

Is There A Solution?

The question is, what can we do, or what are we willing to do, to help correct the evil of disunity (1 Cor. 1:10-13)? Should we approach our neighbors with, 'I'm a Church of Christ; I am not connected with a denomination and everyone should join with me in the one true church?" This is stated less discreetly than it may normally be expressed, but the attitude comes through too often in this way and is resented as narrow, sectarian and Pharisaic. Oftentimes in spite of best intentions, Christians create animosity and spur retaliation, when their motive has been to break down barriers and bring about harmony and peace. What can be done? Is the proposal hopeless? Have disciples of Jesus actually become, to use the words of David Lipscomb, "a sectarian body whose aim it is to fight sectarianism?"

What Are Others Doing?

It may help us to look at what some religious groups have done in the last twenty years to escape the "brand" of their particular religious group. They have learned that most people they approach have a resistance to the idea of going to a church that is different from their own. So what they have been doing with a degree of success, and yet without changing their doctrinal position, is to organize churches under dis-arming non-sectarian names. Graduates from their seminaries have gone out and set up a "Bible Church", a "Christian Center" or a "Living Word" church. They have not abandoned their distinctive traditional doctrines, but operating within the format of a community undenominational church, they have been able to penetrate an unsuspecting populace. The results: their numbers have proliferated rapidly.

If there is any doubt about the success of this movement away from sectarianism, a glance at the yellow page church section in the phone books of most cities will eradicate those doubts. How many "Bible Churches" do you see? How many "Undenominational"? How many "Independent"? How many "Inter-denominational"? And where are the "Church of Christ" and "Church of God"? There they are listed alphabetically along with all the "other" denominations, not among the "undenominational churches"! You will see many more of the "independent" type churches, but few if any more "Churches of Christ or "Churches of God" now than there were twenty years ago.

Another example of what others have done will show some wisdom that we might profitably examine. A very small band of Charles T. Russell's followers with only four members recently placed attractive newspaper ads on several successive days, telling of a film that would be shown about Jesus on a week night at a public hall. They did not give their denominational affiliation, but implied that they were believers in the Bible and in Jesus Christ. The result was that over 700 people attended on that Friday night! Why should not the same approach be made to get a crowd of 700 to hear the pure gospel of Christ?

How could we better practice what we preach about un-sectarian Christianity? Would a good place to start be with the name? We have told our friends that there are many terms by which God's people are known. So why not present to our neighbors a practice that is consistent with what we have been saying? Let us (1) take down "the" name from our buildings and put in its place any name applied to God's people that we find in the Bible . . . if we feel we must have a sign and a building, and (2) let us advertise with any and all biblical names in newspapers, tracts, books, signs, etc. It would be good to assemble as Christians in homes all over the city like they did in the first century, thus aiding the frustration of those who would insist on tacking an exclusive brand on disciples who want to be and do like the early church.

What Is The Church To Be Called?

In an article entitled, "What is the Church to be called," one brother told of a preacher who wished to use a different biblical term when establishing a new mission work. When one editor's opinion was sought, he gave this reply: "The church found in the Scriptures had no proper name . . . any of these terms are Scriptural and can be used." However, the conclusion he gave was, "I could *not* bid him God speed (2 John 9-11) . . . we have enough divisive influences already without such 'pet causes' as this."

It seems unfortunate that a young man should be excluded from the fellowship because he wishes to extend the influence of the gospel by breaking with an exclusively used traditional title, when admittedly there are dozens that could be used and still be within the bounds of Scripture. *Crudens Concordance* has a page that lists over 100 names by which God's people are known.

Applications

Recently three Christians placed an ad in the Fort Worth newspaper, offering to show a Bible film. Anyone desiring to see it was invited to phone or write for information on the times and places it would be shown. No name was given, just phone numbers and a post office box. The response: 75 phone calls the first 3 days, resulting in a dozen showings of the film in both private homes and public halls. Whole households gathered with their friends (one apartment had 17 people waiting and another had 10 adult Catholics), evidently the same as Cornelius who had invited his friends and near kinsmen to hear God's Word (Acts 10). This ad also brought 'out of the woodwork' six men who had left various denominations with a determination to take the Bible as their only guide and the name Christian as their only name . . . men who represented a group of twenty-five people who began meetings in an apartment clubroom. There is little doubt about it: if this advertisement had carried a name like "Baptist" or "Nazarene Church" or "Church of God", likely none of these opportunities would have surfaced. When the people inquired about what church sponsored the film, they were told that it was individual Christians, members of the body of Christ not associated with any denomination. This answer stirred even further inquiry.

Another example: A Bible film on the birth of Christ (Luke 1) and a featured "lecturer" were advertised in the newspaper as a "family forum". As visitors entered the public hall, ushers gave a card to each on which questions could be written and on which their personal needs could be checked. Many opportunities for further study were gained.

Conclusion

When we get out into the market place where the people are, we discover to our surprise that it is not any church that wears a "standard brand" that is reputed to be where the Spirit of the Lord is moving. It is rather in their minds with undenominational independent groups, with charismatics, or with the enthusiastic devotees of some TV personality.

Brothers and sisters we must face these facts. To keep our traditions, we lay aside the Word. Do we refuse to bid godspeed to any brother who prefers not to wear the brand? At the same time, out on the battle fields of immorality and false doctrine we haven't even made an impressive appearance except in a few isolated sectors.

If the reader finds some merit in what he reads, let him become more concerned with wielding the sword of the Spirit and less concerned about displaying "our" flag. Let him do something just a little differently for the sake of dying souls who are lost in sin. Let him be just as broad as the Bible allows him to be, and at the same time be just as narrow as it says he must be. Then he will thank God "who always leads us in triumphal procession in Christ and through us spreads everywhere the fragrance of the knowledge of him" (2 Cor. 2:14).

QUESTIONS

1. What is the most obvious mark of a denomination?

2. Why could Paul not write to the Corinthians as unto spiritual people? (1 Cor. 1:10-13; 3:1-4).

3. What can Christians do in an effort to convince their community that they are not a party, sect or denomination?

4. Can you list a dozen names applied to God's people in the New Testament?

5. Give an example from this chapter of an opportunity to teach where no particular or exclusive name was used.

6. What can we do to show all the world where Jesus' disciples are?- (John 13:35-36).

7. Is it possible that one group may judge another and at the same time condemn itself by practicing the same thing? (Matthew 7:1-5; Romans 7:1).

Why not use all biblical terms rather than any one exclusively or sectarianly?

CHANGEABLE MESSAGE SIGN

[A different Bible name could be displayed every week for over a year without any duplication by using a changeable-letter sign or a computerized changeable message sign.]

We Ought To Be Teachers

13

Hundreds of thousands, or perhaps millions of members of the church of Jesus Christ reside in the great cities of America. This constitutes a vast organism for spreading the good news of the kingdom. As a member youself, you are to teach other faithful men the things you have learned, who will in turn be able to teach others also.[1]

As a member in the body of Christ of several years' standing, by reason of the time you should be a teacher.[2] You may feel there is no need for you to teach inasmuch as you feel there are "enough teachers already for each of the classes at church." This reflects a vastly different definition of teaching than what we have in mind. It also indicates a view that what teaching there is to be done is to be at the church house. But look again at your Bible. *Where was the classroom then?* Wherever it was then is where it ought to be today. Out there where the people are is where God wants us to be teaching, winning, pleading, reconciling. In the eyes of the world the wise man is the prudent businessman or the skilled diplomat or the astute philosopher; but in the eyes of the Lord, "he that winneth souls is wise."[3] We must be burdened with the lost of the world like our Lord was.[4]

The early church, the model church, was composed

of men and women who were driven from their homes and their kin and who "went everywhere preaching the word."[5] Yet, so many of us sit in our smugness, indifference and complacency with our "You can come and get it if you want it" attitude.

Our field is white, ready for reapers to come and take the harvest.[6] Prospects are unlimited and opportunities are at every hand. An unknown writer describes the dying church in these lines:

> "Our potential is limitless. We must arise!! Someone has written, 'A church that does not extend to meet opportunities and possibilities is on its way to the cemetery. The members who do nothing are its pallbearers. All who are busy with their own affairs and have no time for the church carry the wreath. The indifferent brother is driving the hearse. Those always holding the church back are throwing flowers on the grave. The brother who is always saying, 'It can't be done,' is preaching the funeral, and the grumblers are singing the hymns. Thus the church dies from all cares.' "

Let us never forget that every branch in Christ that "beareth not fruit he taketh away."[7] We cannot afford to come before our Master at the day of judgment with the blood stains on our hands from the lost whom we might have reached but did not.[8]

Choose Your Method

You can choose the method of instruction that you know how to use and that suits you best. You can use one or more of these teaching methods: (1) With an open Bible teach another person in their home or yours. (2) Use Bible films and cassettes. (3) Gather a group together and invite a guest speaker or teacher to help you. (4) Take your friends and acquaintances to public meetings where able evangelists can be heard. (5) Distribute tracts and gospel magazines with your contact address offering further instruction and help. (6) Visit meetings of religious people and seek opportunity to speak out. (7) Use Bible charts. You can specialize in any one method or engage in all, and even add other methods.

105

Paul became weak to the weak, and became all things to people of all sorts that he might "BY ALL MEANS" save some and that he might be a sharer of the good news with others.[9]

Facts About The Plan

The divine plan of evangelizing stands on a foundation of combined (1) direct teaching and (2) indirect teaching. Both of these are equally important, both equally essential to the success of reaching every creature as well as to your own success as a teacher. It is stated in the Bible in these words:

> "And the things you have heard me say in the presence of many witnesses entrust to reliable men who will also be qualified to teach others."[10]

The divine writer here gave the command to teach the gospel directly to faithful men, and these men in turn would be able to pass the message on to others. A failure on the second phase of this charge is what causes churches to flourish when an able evangelist is serving them. Their ability consists of baptizing those he has personally taught and there the evangelism stops. When he personally is pushing there is progress, but because of his human limitations and weakness his ministry must be classified as only partially successful. He has failed if he has not deposited the message in the hands of other men who are qualified and motivated to become teachers also.

On the other hand, only partial success is attained when a Christian teacher only urges others to reach out to the lost into the homes and hiways and byways,[11] when he himself will not do any direct teaching to the lost.

The wise Christian is acutely aware of the necessity to maintain a balance between direct personal teaching and training the instructed one to become a teacher also. He sets goals and dreams dreams that he's a little bit scared of, to make him stretch and to make him grow. For example, he may strive to present the gospel to ten lost souls per month, in addition to meeting personally at least five times a month with his converts until they have proved themselves as "teachers also."

Sharing With The Instructor

When goals are set, the evangelist, pastor or teacher must expect to spend many hours in the preparation and delivery of his lessons. He will also spend much time in prayer and in developing interest and setting up study appointments. His principle motivation for preaching and teaching is to serve God, but he knows he cannot give himself to "laboring in the word" unless some financial help is received from it. He will be able to donate several hours each week and is glad to do so, but if he is dreaming of becoming more and more fruitful in the Lord's work, he has a right to expect support from it. Note these passages from his Book of rules, the Bible:

> "Anyone who receives instruction in the word must share all good things with his instructor." Gal. 6:6 NIV

> "Soldiers don't pay their own wages. A farmer who plants a grape field is allowed to eat some of the grapes. A shepherd who takes care of the flock of sheep gets some of the milk from the flock . . . Since we planted spiritual things among you, it should be no big thing to harvest physical things from you . . . In the same way the Lord Jesus commanded that the men who are preaching the Good News should be able to make a living from preaching it." 1 Cor. 9:7,11,14 SEB

> "Christ appointed apostles, prophets, evangelists, shepherds and teachers to prepare holy people for a ministry of service, for building up the body of Christ."
> Eph. 4:11 SEB

As we reflect on the services of teaching performed in the churches through the years, both to the alien and to the members of the body of Christ, in how many instances was there any sharing of good things by the instructed with the teacher of the good news? Normally only the public proclaimer, *"the preacher"* of the congregation, is supported in his work and his principle functioning in most instances centers at the church building. If there ever was a plan carried out to support a teacher by those who were instructed by him, it must have been a closely guarded secret for this writer never has known of it during the forty years he has been a member of the church. And is this at least part of the reason that laborers are so few? They are not rewarded for their labors; they have not been partakers of the good things of those whom they instructed. Paul asked the forgiveness of the congregation at Corinth for his doing wrong in causing them to be inferior to the rest of the churches. His fault was not that he had failed to teach them the gospel, nor that he had shirked or been negligent in his ministry among them. To the contrary, he said that he did not come "behind even the chiefest of the apostles, though I am nothing," laboring among them with steadfastness, "by signs and wonders and mighty works."[12] He had spent himself and said he would gladly do so again when he returned. But his fault was that he did not allow them to support him, he did not become a burden to them. He hastened to say, "I seek not yours, but you: for the children ought not to lay up for the parents, but the parents for the children." He (as their father in the gospel) by loving them more and spending himself fully as a parent would naturally do, had been "loved the less" by those to whom he most completely devoted himself. He called it a "wrong" (Greek, an "unrighteousness," *adikian*).

Although we do not believe preachers preach just for the money, still if the support was not there for them, many would be forced to enter some other type work to feed and clothe their families. Godliness is not to be supposed as a way of gain,[13] and those who are motivated to preach by the hope of financial gain have their reward. But neither is it right that those who labor in the gospel should be deprived of living of it. That is plain Bible teaching. There would be many more elders doing the work God appointed them to do if they were supported in it as God says they should be when they labor in the word. "The laborer is worthy of his hire."[14]

Special Needs Vs. Ministry Support

A great deal has been said about the contribution of 1 Corinthians 16:1-2. Is this the pattern for financing the ministry of the word as well as benevolence? In reading the New Testament through and observing how workers were supported, would it appear that those who were taught made their gift directly to the teacher or shepherd without regard for when or where, and that the contributions on the Lord's days were for special needs? Some have observed that from Abraham through the entire Bible the gift was given to the man of God primarily for his sustenance. Other offerings were for various purposes and needs. Check it out in your Bible. *Logia* (Greek) in 1 Corinthians 16:1-2 is "a special collection" from the regular gifts of Christians.[15]

James Robert Jarrell, minister of a church in Missouri, writes:

"In 1 Corinthians 9:4-18, Paul affirms the right of Christian workers to be supported. He writes, 'Do we not have the right to our food and drink? Do we not have the right to be accompanied by a wife, as the other apostles and the brothers of the Lord and Cephas? Or is it only Barnabas and I who have no right to refrain from working for a living?' Then in verses 8-11, Paul gives some reasons why apostles and the brothers of Christ should receive material support.

These reasons for supporting apostles and certain others apply equally, of course, to ALL who work for the church. Paul specifically applies it to preachers in verses 13-14: 'Do you not know that those who are employed in the temple service get their food from the temple, and those who serve at the altar share in the sacrificial offerings? In the same way, *the Lord commanded that those who proclaim the gospel should get their living by the gospel.*'

Financial or material support for elders is specifically commanded in 1 Timothy 5:17-18 and for teachers in Galatians 6:6. See also Matthew 10:9-10 and Philippians 4:15-18.

109

There were times when Paul refused to accept financial support (Acts 17:3; 20:34; 1 Corinthians 9:12, 15-18; 1 Thessalonians 2:9; 2 Thessalonians 3:7-11), even though he had the *right* to receive it.

It is my often-stated view that it is wiser for a congregation to have *two* "professionally-trained" *elders* (pastors) who have full financial support from the congregation *instead of* having a preacher/minister — or, at least, *before* they have a preacher/minister. The usual system that is presently used is unwieldy, awkward, and inefficient, in my view — even though it is Scriptural. If this change takes place, it would probably occur during a snow storm in July in Texas."[16]

We would not expect the change to occur soon which brother Jarrell describes, nor does he expect it. While the change he describes is not what we are advocating, it is nevertheless a step in the same direction.

The changes we would like to see as described in this book may not be seen in our lifetime. One said it would take 300 years. Another said, "a clean break would have to come with the 'institutional church' to accomplish it, unless God works a miracle." But we have enough confidence in God and in our great brotherhood of Christians to believe that God will through them do *abundantly above* what these have thought, because of the power that works in us!

Starting Right

The proven way to teach the word to friends, relatives and neighbors is to start with confidence. You have the assurance that you are backed by the guarantee of heaven itself as you teach the gospel without addition or subtraction. Jesus promised He would be with you wherever you go, providing you teach only the things that He taught.[17] Remember to keep your eye open particularly for "able men who will be able to teach others also."[18] They can go places you cannot go and reach souls you cannot reach, but you must help them get started in living for Christ and in equipping them as a teacher.

Working The Plan

There is no short-cut to establishing yourself as a good minister of Christ Jesus. Rather you must prove by experience as others have done, that you will hold the confidence of those you are striving to teach simply by the attention you give them. The good will and reputation for fairness to them and to God that you will build up is far more important to them than any artificial rules or restrictions that anyone might establish for you. The Christian teacher will never lack for opportunities to share the message if the quality of his service matches the quality of the product he is presenting. This is a basic principle in secular business as well as in the Lord's business. Jesus came to earth to do "His Father's business" and He carried it out to the end in a responsible, business-like manner.[19] We should be like our Master.[20]

A Covenant Relationship

When a person accepts Jesus Christ in loving and faithful obedience, he enters into a contractual covenant relationship. A covenant is an agreement between two parties where one party makes the terms of the agreement and the other party accepts those terms. When we became a Christian, we came into a covenant relationship with God on His terms given through His Son, Jesus Christ. We agreed to yield our lives to Him as slaves who had been bought with a price. The price paid for us by God shows how valuable we are to Him. The price was the blood of His only Son.[21] We are thenceforth not our own because we have been bought with a price, a great price.[22] Jesus made us, but afterward we strayed away from Him. He loved us and bought us back again even though we were unworthy. He gave us His New Covenant to furnish us instructions for everything we need in life and godliness.[23]

When this concept is properly explained to the prospective child of God, he will understand that when he believes and is baptized he will be saved, but that this is

111

only the beginning. This is a new birth into an entirely new relationship, a new family. With this understanding, he will be prepared to give whatever time or resources he has that may be requested by his Lord. He is not his own.

If you understand this to be your relationship to God through Christ, and if you are able to impart this to others, you are now ready to begin.

QUESTIONS

1. What key passage teaches a "direct" and indirect teaching responsibility?

2. Can you name 5 different methods of teaching the lost?

3. What methods would you suggest for "sharing your physical things" with your teacher? Does your answer coincide with a biblical example?

4. Does the shepherd have bad motives by expecting to get some milk from his flock?

5. How did Paul wrong the Corinthians whom he had taught the gospel?

6. Have you entered a covenant relationship with King Jesus?

FOOTNOTES

[1] 2 Timothy 2:2
[2] Hebrews 5:12
[3] Proverbs 11:30
[4] Luke 19:41
[5] Acts 8:4
[6] John 4:35
[7] John 15:2
[8] Ezekiel 33:7-9
[9] 1 Corinthians 9:22-23
[10] 2 Timothy 2:2 (NIV)
[11] Luke 14:23
[12] 2 Corinthians 12:11-16
[13] 1 Timothy 6:5
[14] 1 Timothy 5:17-18; Luke 10:7; 1 Corinthians 9:14
[15] Wm. Barclay, p. 181, quoted by Burton Coffman, Commentary on 1 & 2 Corinthians, p. 276.
[16] Views & News, Dec. 24, 1980. Vol. 9, No. 21.
[17] Matthew 28:18-20
[18] 2 Timothy 2:2
[19] Luke 2:49
[20] Romans 12:11; 1 Corinthians 11:1
[21] Eph. 1:7; Acts 20:28; Heb. 13:12; Rev. 1:5
[22] 1 Corinthians 6:20; 7:23; 1 Peter 3:4
[23] 2 Timothy 3:16-17

Arithmetic
On Teacher's
Support

14

Most teachers of the gospel begin on a part-time basis with a limited group of friends and relatives. They will gradually supplement this nucleus by a list of prospective learners, a list that can be developed by door-to-door contact, by referrals, by telephone, by literature, by "reasoning in the market place," etc.

Some are men and some are women, but most will be husband and wife partnerships. The majority are hardworking people like yourself. Some will be young people starting a lifetime career, some will be retired folk with incomes supplemented by various part-time endeavors, plus some business and professional people. They have all been blessed materially, some more than others, but they all have one thing in common though they may not realize it; there is a void in their life that can only be fulfilled by Christ.

There should be no hesitance nor embarrassment about telling them their duty and privilege in supporting you as their teacher. That is the subject of this chapter, and that is a part of the good news. They can actually become partners with God in doing His work! When they are counting the cost of discipleship, they need to weigh whether they are willing (1) to live a pure life for Christ on a day to day basis,[1] (2) to assemble with other Christians on the first day of each week,[2] (3) to teach others,[3] and (4) to give a portion of their financial prosperity to their teacher for Christ and His church.[4]

Any time any gift has been given to God (from the earliest paying of tithes by Abraham to Melchizedek[5]) the gift has been put into the hand of another man. If a congregation takes up a collection, the money given to God is put into the hand of someone, usually a treasurer, who deposits it in a bank for disbursing under the supervision of the elders. If you have been authorized to teach or preach or shepherd by a commission from God through His Word and/or by the overseers of the church where you live, it would be a biblical practice for you to so teach the new or prospective Christian. He then could be expected to give into your hand a portion of his prosperity. You in turn would carry this gift to the treasurer of the church for deposit. Below is a simple diagram of this procedure where there were two families whom you are teaching and with whom you are assembling for worship each Lord's day:

Teacher's Support By Those Instructed

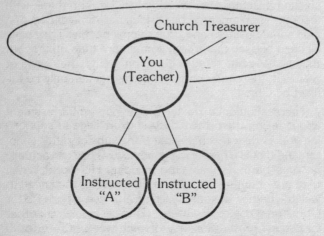

Diagram #5

These Lord's Day meetings would be conducted in the home of one of the families being instructed, or in your own home. The contribution from the two persons being instructed together with your contribution would be taken to the treasurer, a faithful brother appointed to this work by the elders in the city. The elders would also determine an appropriate portion to return for the support of the teacher. The church's other functions such as public hall rental, radio - TV evangelism, literature, Bibles, benevolence, foreign evangelism, etc. are financed in part by the surplus as well as by special gifts and offerings of love.

If you are only teaching two others we would see something like this on a dollar basis if each contributed 10% and if you also contributed 10%. This proportion should be taught as a minimum goal for God's people of all ages. If we use this figure for some basic arithmetic, and if each of the three families receives near minimum wage, the week's earnings and gifts could then be figured as shown here:

Your wage, $150	Your gift	$15
Instructed A's wage $150	A's gift	$15
Instructed B's wage, $150	B's gift	$15
	Total	$45

If the national averages hold true among those whom you instruct, half of the men will have a wage-earning wife. This would mean that your gift together with the gifts from "A" and "B" would be about $67.50.

Increased Opportunities!

As you continue to work with "A" and "B," you are helping them as heads of their families to instruct their wives and children to live according to the Bible. If you are faithful in serving the spiritual needs of "A" and "B," they will grow and in the process of time God will give you more responsibility and opportunities to teach. Jesus taught this in the parable of the talents. The faithful and wise steward increased his master's goods and received commendation, rewards and additional opportunities (talents) from him.[6] The application of Jesus' lesson to our study is that when we use what abilities he has given us, he will reward us and call us "good and faithful servants." He will then give us more opportunities of serving and teaching. If your opportunities are doubled, as in the parable, your situation would be:

1. Your wage, $150	gift	$15
2. Instructed A's wage, $150		15
3. Instructed B's wage, $150		15
4. Instructed C's wage, $150		15
5. Instructed D's wage, $150		15
	Total	$75
Add one half for wives' gifts		37.50
	Total	$112.50

The elders will award you according to your needs and your fruitfulness by biblical and right standards.[7] They know the laborer is worthy of his hire. No one can justly criticize you nor your overseers for compensating you. If your overseers approve your attitude and motivation, you may desire to quit your regular job and give your full time to the proclamation of the gospel. You will need to develop a group of ten to fifteen families for you to be sustained by their contributions.

Diagram #6

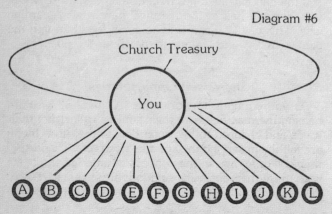

Not a True Picture

According to Paul's charge to Timothy, his child in the faith, the diagram on page 116 is *not an accurate portrayal of the evangelist's ministry,* if he is "fulfilling his ministry" and properly doing the work of an evangelist. It only takes into account *one half* of the charge given in 2 Timothy 2:2. Do you see the defect? Though it is a distorted picture, it nevertheless does portray what actually occurs in many churches today where "the preacher" may be the only one who is reaching out and converting the lost. The moment he relaxes, the growth levels off or begins to decline. He has failed in half of his ministry. Even Jesus would have failed had He not trained faithful men to be teachers of what He had taught them.

"Fireball" Evangelist or "Average Dude"

Would it be better for a super-evangelistic "fireball" to teach and baptize one person per day 365 days a year, or for an average "dude" like you or me to teach and train only one person a year who himself becomes a discipler? Which would bear greater fruit over a period of 25 years? Remember that the discipler who teaches and trains only one other person each year to become what his teacher is, will multiply and reproduce himself at the rate we shall project at one each year:

In 5 years:	"Fireball" has gained	1825
	"Average Dude" has gained	32
In 13 years:	"Fireball" has gained	4745
	"Average Dude" has gained	8192
In 25 years:	"Fireball" has gained	9125
	"Average Dude" has gained	33,554,432

It is obvious that the discipling ministry is the multiplying ministry.

Jesus worked intimately with twelve men for about three years to implant in them the knowledge, the ability and the desire to carry on His work after He was no longer with them. It is doubtful that you alone can effectively train twelve men like He did, but you may be able to train four who will be able to teach others also.

117

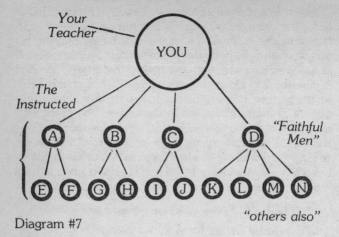

Diagram #7

This is a true diagram of 2 Timothy 2:2, so far as you are concerned. You teach A, B, C, and D; they instruct the "others also" identified above as "E" through "N", now a total of more than a dozen men. You do not directly teach "E" through "N" unless A, B, C or D ask you to help them. It may be easier for you to teach them all "direct," but that is not what the passage states.

Know By Fruit

Jesus said men are to be known by their fruit.[8] When the elders see a faithful brother has reached a certain degree of fruitfulness (see "D" in diagram), coupled with Christ-like attitudes and motivations, they may ask him to serve as a full-time servant of the Lord with full support from the church. Being freed from working with his hands, his fruit-bearing will increase all the more to the praise of God's glory and to the harvesting of an abundance of precious souls.

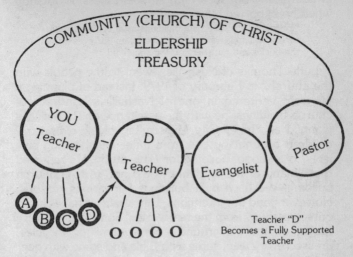

Diagram #8

This diagram presents a view of the entire community of Christ. Its growth potential is unlimited and the financial resources go almost wholly into the preaching of the gospel. In congregations where the one man "pastor system" prevails, or where the bulk of preaching and teaching is by "the preacher" whose labors are centered in a church-owned building, a large portion of the contributions must go to the purchase of the land and building and its maintenance. It requires from 150 to 200 members of the body of Christ to support one full-time minister on an average where a church property is involved.

It Will Work Today

A full-time worker is supported by only 27 members in one religious group where no church-owned property is involved.[9]

Roger Woodward, elder in Enid, Oklahoma, was right in addressing Sunset's Fifth Annual Elders' Workshop when he exhorted fellow elders:

> "I think our big beautiful buildings have become a detriment to us elderships. We have taken our eyes off of the flocks and put them on the sheepfold."[10]

Lytle Thomas of Nashville, "went to the people with the church" in February of 1979. Instead of planning a program centered in one of Nashville's hundreds of church buildings, he with the assistance of 31 churches planned an "Inner City Ministry" involving over 1,000 children brought by bus from inner city housing projects to a school building for Bible study. He reported that "many of the students would not go to a church building. We have built buildings for various reasons. However good our intentions, I am afraid we have closed ourselves away from the real world." Some classes were taught on the playgrounds. Some came on bicycles, dressed every way, some with Bible and some with beer in hand.[11]

Another example of the workability of "outside" evangelism has been reported from Kentucky where Don Peden and one other family began meeting in 1980 in a big old house in the inner city. From this handful of faithful Christians as a nucleus, God gave increase to nearly a hundred in attendance within a few weeks time. Many 'unchurched' people have become interested in the gospel as well as several students from the nearby university.

One brother, Kelly Lawson, taught and baptized 135 souls in a lake in the heart of Dallas in 1978 — and all meetings were right in the apartment complex where the people lived. It *can* happen today! It *has* happened today! Here are brother Lawson's words:

> "I dropped by the apartment house that Glenn Alexander owned off Cedar Springs and met with Don Tutor who was a member of the church, and also with the manager of the apartments. I had the opportunity to study with her and her fiance;

they obeyed the gospel. Her two teenage children obeyed the gospel from her influence. The assistant manager obeyed the gospel, some of the maintenance people there in the apartment house obeyed the gospel and we baptized them in Bachman's Lake. We have pictures of that. Then the original group who had been meeting and studying together with the idea of teaching them to observe all things, they began to teach others.

We have a program of asking every one that we meet if they are a Christian. If they answer, "yes," we say, "wonderful, fantastic; we are really glad to know that. Where do you worship? We would be honored to have you come and study with us and worship with us some Sunday." If they are not a Christian, we tell them that we would be happy to have them come and visit with us. We play up Jesus and play down church buildings. We claim the church is the true body of God's believers. We have found that people in the world are very positive toward Jesus Christ and very negative toward what they consider organized religion. As these people begin to recognize the truth found in the New Testament their feelings surface about organized religion and its hypocrisy. That makes them even more enthusiastic about spreading the word."

Evangelism in the marketplace has been almost totally neglected in our times, despite the fact that Paul and his companions met every day in marketplaces to reason with the people concerning Jesus Christ (Acts 17:17). Why not set up a table at each of the thousands of "flea markets" across the country and reach out to the masses with Bibles, tracts, cassettes, etc.?[12]

Weighed And Found Wanting

More and more evangelists, pastors and teachers are advocating a new examination of the Scriptures with reference to evangelism and the use of church funds. Have expensive urban properties been weighed and found wanting in that they have taken away millions of dollars annually from world evangelism? How many aspiring men have been turned away in their efforts to raise support because of a building program? Something is vastly lacking when Christians cannot find support for those who are willing to go abroad to preach the gospel. We now support only one full-time worker (at home or abroad) per 150 members, whereas another religious group supports 1 out of 27. Why can we not do the same and increase missions support through the home-shepherding arrangement? Look what could be done from 50,000 members in the D/FW area alone:

Example A: We could have 2,000 full-time workers at home, not 350 as we now have, or

Example B: We could have 700 workers at home (that's double the present number) PLUS 700 missionary families supported at *twice* the amount. This is more missionaries than are now serving from our entire brotherhood.

Example C: Growth in the metro would probably grow to double within 5 years, thus doubling the missions potential as well.

When Building Expansion Is Necessary

If a congregation is blessed with good leaders and a committed group of praying and working members, numerical growth will be inevitable. But along with the joy and gratitude comes a realization that the building can no longer contain the crowds. This need can be met in part by the multiple use of the auditorium and classroom areas, but that may already have been done. What then? The mortgage on the last addition may still be unpaid, and the goal of sending more funds to the mission fields when the mortgage is met, has still not been realized. And now it seems another building program must be initiated.

This is the history of congregation "x". First a $250,000 building and property were purchased in 1960. A larger auditorium costing $400,000 was added ten years later, when the older space was all converted to classrooms. Then in 1975 more classrooms, a fellowship hall and an expanded parking area were added at an additional $300,000. Now the facility is crowded to its limits and the cycle needs to be repeated. The skyrocketing building costs will necessitate spending much more than they did six years ago, and now more land must be acquired from adjacent landowners. It is common to hear of a million dollar expansion, and one congregation is now selling bonds for a five million dollar addition.

Is this a familiar story in your city? Churches can get off this treadmill! They can combine the use of their present facility with home-shepherding and put the next half million dollars "into all the world." Come now

Diagram #9

EXPANSION TREADMILL

brethren and let us reason together! *Read* the Bible; consider this *writin* and *rithmetic* and launch out by faith in the direction of Jerusalem. Don't you really think its time has come? Lyle Shaller of Yokefellow Institute estimates there are "at least 25,000" churches meeting in homes in the U.S.A. and Canada, and "probably closer to 50,000." They are most frequently found in the inner city and in rural German farming areas.[13]

J.C. Bailey of India reported in June of 1984 that there were some 50 places where disciples were meeting in the city of Vijayawada alone, all converts within the last 20 years. There had been no divisions but there were that many places where a meeting was held and the converts simply continued meetings where they were. A brother Enoch worked diligently to get 20 of these groups to come together into 7 congregations to study about elders. They then did appoint elders in each of these larger congregations. As we search the New Testament, do we find any precedent for this procedure? When these larger groups were brought together, this would necessitate some regular place larger than private houses for each crowd to assemble and obviously substantial sums of money for funding them. Why should not these 50 groups have remained where they were in their regular weekly assemblies, and faithful men from each group come together to consider the possibility of appointing elders in the city for the church in Vijayawada? Although this would be a departure from the customary manner of church leadership in America, it would avoid the development of a multiplicity of elderships in the city — for which there is no biblical record. Upon certain occasions the "whole church" could all come together under their one leadership.

Look To The Fields

Look for a moment to the fields abroad, those remote places where the gospel has not been proclaimed. When a man and his family go to one of those distant cities, he will begin teaching in his home and in the homes of the people. He will probably next move meetings to a rented hall, at least for occasional evangelistic efforts. During those first years, the precentage growth will be very rapid. The going will be tough while he carves out from a heathen population a people for God's own possession and to wear His Name.

When that process begins to work and the new converts are beginning to be added, the missionary begins to think, "Now we need to buy a building but these few are not in a position to furnish funds for the kind of property that will be a worthy tribute to the Cause we espouse. We will launch a fund-raising campaign among Christians of America to buy us a building like they have." And so they do. It is at that point that we see the beginning of a decline in growth rate, and after the building is erected in the next two to five years, the growth levels off and especially if there is sufficient financial support to take care of the preacher in this "self-supporting" church.

A strong move is underway now among our people to erect a million-dollar building on a main street of every major city in many nations abroad, "to show the people of those nations that we are there to stay and that we are no 'fly-by-night' bunch!" While the intentions are not questioned, may we pause to ask, "Is this the pattern for evangelizing you read in the Book of Acts?" It rather looks like the period of Constantine when the church passed out of the hard days to the easy ways of being a respectable, recognized institution with wealth and prestige. Can't we learn from history, if not from the Bible, that God's strength is in man's weakness? These dazzling attractions appeal to the material minded carnal man. While numbers may be attracted they will not likely be the caliber that were won *solely* through lifting up Jesus Christ and Him crucified amidst trial, persecution and hardship. We wonder if every missionary, looking back at his experience on the field, would not say that the best growth rate numerically and spiritually was in the early period, before an attempt was put forth to buy property and imitate the American pattern of church development. When did the levelling off period begin? It was probably when the second stage of 2 Timothy 2:2 was not developed, and attention was given to how to hold the people in one place so the one teacher — evangelist could continue his direct teaching activity. The natural answer is a big building larger than a private dwelling, and that meant leaving the word ministry to engage in fund raising and management of a property. This writer spent 15 years following this pattern in repeated efforts in foreign large cities, when as a young man there seemed to be no alternative. Now he sees another way, a way that excites every foreign evangelist with a prospect of more support for his work if these principles are applied in America where God has entrusted so great a potential to His servants for a world outreach.

QUESTIONS

1. How can an instructed person learn about his obligation to his instructor?

2. Should a person begin teaching without a commission by an eldership? Why?

3. Discuss the tithe as a new covenant standard of giving.

4. What deficiency in the ministry is portrayed in diagram #6?

5. Can you give an example of a modern conversion experience that involved scores of souls who never came into a church property?

6. Can a young man more easily picture himself as a preacher who addresses a vast audience of 1,000, or as a teacher of a dozen or two in a private dwelling?

FOOTNOTES

[1] Galatians 2:20
[2] Hebrews 10:25
[3] Matthew 28:18
[4] Galatians 6:6; 1 Corinthians 16:1-2
[5] Genesis 14:18; Hebrews 7:1-4
[6] Matthew 25:14-30
[7] Galatians 6:6-7
[8] Matthew 7:20
[9] This denomination in 5 years grew to over 400 members with 8 full-time pastors besides several part-time workers and liberal support for missionaries.
[10] Quoted from "Let's Go Back Home and Tend the Flock," Tape 8A, 1980, Sunset School of Preaching Extension, Lubbock, Texas.
[11] Lytle Thomas, "His Church Goes To The People," *The World Evangelist*, Feb. 1983 issue. Basil Overton, editor, Florence, AL.
[12] For a report on techniques and responses to recent efforts in flea-market teaching, see "Evangelism In The Marketplace," 15-minute narrated filmstrip by Alvin Jennings, Star Bible, Ft. Worth, TX.
[13] Personal letter, May 1984.

The Work Of An Evangelist

15

S ome may be asking, "But where does the evangelist fit into the picture? Is there *no pulpit* from which he can herald the gospel?"

We have seen from another chapter what the work of the teacher is and how "you should have become teachers a long time ago."[1] We observed some of the reasons there are so few teachers of God's word today. In another place we observed the elder (pastor, overseer, shepherd) and his relationship to the people under his oversight, and how spiritual men often "shepherd", "feed", "nurture" others even though they may not be qualified for the office of elder.[2]

How Beautiful Upon The Mountains!

Among the greatest men of God are those who feel the joy and compulsion to tell the Good News to those who have not heard. They are likened to the messenger who has run with great speed with news of a victory in battle, who reaching a mountain-top and breathless from exhaustion, shouts loudly from afar to the people who eagerly await his coming.[3] How beautiful are their feet upon the mountains!

Jeremiah expressed the absolute necessity of telling men the word of God when he said there was a "fire" burning in his bones, so that he could not hold it back![4]

127

He had become so discouraged when only a few would listen to what God spoke through him, that he resolved to quit preaching. But when he tried, he could not quit. He had to go and tell it. He was hated, threatened, and thrown into a deep and miry dungeon to die. But still he proclaimed to the king and all those under him, the judgments and decrees of the Almighty. The preacher speaks the truth even when the people will not obey.[5]

The obligation to tell good news when it is known is powerfully portrayed in 2 Kings, chapter seven where some lepers learned of an abundance of food that was available *free* to a starving city. When they ate their fill and hid what they wanted, they realized their obligation to go quickly and tell the people in the city who were perishing with hunger, lest they be punished for their neglect.[6] A powerful sermon on cassette by evangelist Avon Malone is available from the publisher on this text.

Jerusalem's Evangelists

Two of the most courageous heralds of the gospel were Philip and Stephen. These men were "full of wisdom and full of the Holy Spirit."[7] Philip's work can be traced through Acts 8 and other places. Stephen spoke with such wisdom and power that the Jews could not argue with him, so they seized him and took him before their Council and made false charges against him. As they stared at him his face shined like an angel and when he opened his mouth to speak, the truths he quoted from the scriptures and applied to their lives (see Acts chapter 7) sank deeply into their hearts and consciences. But instead of obeying the truth and repenting, they became angry and killed him as he was praying that God would be merciful to them.

These men of conviction, empowered through the Holy Spirit, were members of the Jerusalem church. We don't know how many others there were like them, but whoever they were and wherever they went, they "preached the word."[8] The concept of a large comfortable building with an elevated pulpit stand in front of many rows of padded pews does not come to mind as you read about evangelists in the Jerusalem church, does it? Where was Philip's pulpit? Where was Stephen's? Was it not where their Master's had been? Was it not in the streets, the hiways, the homes, the marketplaces, the Jews' synagogues, before magistrates, councils, and rulers?

God Put Evangelists In The Church

God put evangelists in the church.[9] There are only three references in the New Testament to the evangelist (Acts 21:8; Eph. 4:11; 2 Tim. 4:5). The noun form (*euangelion*) means "glad tidings, good or joyful news," and is commonly referred to as "gospel", found seventy times in the New Testament. In the verb form, it appears over fifty times. A parallel word, to preach (*kerussein*) "to proclaim or herald" is found over sixty times. To preach the gospel is clearly a major function of the New Testament church.[10]

The apostles were essentially evangelists, commissioned by Christ on numerous occasions to go and preach. They were determined to concentrate on the ministry of the Word, so appointed others to look after other tasks in the church.[11]

Their Task

The evangelists had a specific job and place in the church, along with the apostles, prophets, pastors and teachers.[12] Their goal was "the building up of the body of Christ" both in numerical increase and in nurtured strength. When the apostolic office and the prophetic office disappeared, the full weight of their *outreach leadership* would fall on the evangelists.[13]

Every Member Evangelism

Since Jesus Christ came pre-eminently "preaching",[14] it is not surprising to find an "every member evangelism" in the early church.[15] Disciples will be like their master, their teacher, their mentor. They will naturally tell the good news wherever they go since their Master was a teller of good news. "As you are going into all the world, you will preach the gospel to every creature." This is a literal rendering of the commission as recorded in Mark's gospel.[16] Even though evangelizing was a church-wide function and permeated the thinking and speaking of all the members, the tone and standard of this work was set by those who concentrated their energies and qualified their lives by an inner compulsion to lead out on a full-time basis in seeking the lost. These men were called evangelists.

Church Growth And Evangelism

When there is a failure to preserve the *every member evangelism* and the specific office and function of the evangelist, the inevitable consequence will be a decline in numerical growth. The history of post-apostolic Christianity has a marked absence of the evangelist. Then with the conversion of Constantine in A.D. 313, and the attendant change in attitudes toward the church, people flowed into the church more through conforming to what was socially respectable than through evangelism.

Decline In Missionary Activity

Missionary activity is the thrust of evangelism to other lands, other people and other language groups. When internal politics became a greater concern for the church than missionary outreach, it found itself incapable of converting Islamic, Barbaric, Mormon or other invaders. Other means will be employed to attract by material embellishments or to enforce by the sword. By these means, outsiders may become "Christians"; this will result in big numbers but an attending demonstration of spiritual poverty. Geoffrey Ellis comments on the Restoration Movement as having only recently received evangelism as a central emphasis, and adds:

"The movement also has had difficulty in breaking out of the preacher-minister stereotype of Protestantism which incorrectly assigns the pastoral function to the preacher rather than to the elder. Only slowly has the practice of the doctrine of the evangelistic congregation gained momentum among the adherents to restoration-ism even in this twentieth century."[17]

Evangelistic Fervor Restored

The loss of our evangelistic fervor is evidenced by our lack of numerical growth. If we tell the story often in a spirit of love, God will give increase accordingly. But if we continue to sow sparingly, we shall continue to experience a meager harvest of souls.[18] When the scattering of the seed is widespread into all kinds of soils, some will through God's providence find their way into "honest and good hearts."[19] When Kelly Lawson was asked how 1200 prisoners could be baptized within one year in the Dallas County Jail, he replied, "There was no magic formula. There was a divine formula. We found that when we taught more people, we baptized more people; when we taught fewer, we baptized fewer. It was that simple. We taught the truth plainly to as many as possible, and God gave the increase. It was the same in apartment evangelism where we baptized 135 within a year's time. We taught daily, and those who were taught became enthusiastic and began to teach others. We never assembled in a church building with a sign on it, but God formed a community of believers with meetings right where they were in one of the vacant apartments."

The spirit and excitement of seeing the Lord work through His word is phenomenal when people have no feeling of being proselyted into a particular sect or denomination. Most of the barriers that have been erected by creeds and catechisms written by men are broken down by a Christian with evangelistic enthusiasm going with his *Bible only* to show how folk can become *Christians only*.

Three Outreach Emphases

The Neighborhood. Evangelism in the immediate neighborhood is greatly enhanced by conducting assemblies in private homes. The meetings themselves will arouse interest among the neighbors and give occasion for questions to be asked and for answers to be given.[20] A convenient and natural atmosphere is developed which places Christ and His body of believers within reach of the people next door. When they see our worship each Lord's day, we shall be "proclaiming the Lord's death till he come."[21] This is evangelism.

The City. When men who have distinguished themselves as preachers of the gospel are passing through our area, they should be invited to speak at large gatherings. Or capable men from our own area could herald the message on such occasions, men like Stephen or Philip or Peter in the Jerusalem church. The rental of a large hall or theater is arranged for the occasion and all the city is invited to attend. This is the type of meeting described in Acts, chapter twenty.

The fellowship of the smaller group is supplemented by these larger gatherings, thus combining the unique advantages and qualities of both the "little church" and the "big church."

The World. Evangelists who have been on missionary journeys to distant lands will eagerly anticipate the time when they can return and rehearse to the church what God has done with them.[22] They will not feel they are beggars or intruders when they tell how God has opened doors among the heathen, and when they tell of needs for financial support in continuing and enlarging their labors. Their appeals will not be given second-rate consideration, because the basic design and purpose of all the church's function is world evangelism. It is therefore in the position of highest priority, and to fill the needs of the evangelist is their highest honor.[23]

It cannot be denied that one of the missionary's most

frequent hindrances to raising the necessary personal and working funds is the "building program" back home. Many young men have become discouraged and have lost their zeal for going into all the world because they could not find a church that would send them (see Rom. 10:13-18). They often get a job and go back into secular work, while their home church and other churches they have approached plan additions to their facilities or while they pay off the mortgage they already have.

Brethren, there is an alternative. The night is far spent, but it is not too late to arise and evangelize our neighborhood, our city, our world.

QUESTIONS

1. What is the significance of "How beautiful upon the mountains are the feet . . . . ?"

2. Which prophet resolved to quit preaching, but could not?

3. Who said, "We do not well: this day is a day of good tidings, and we hold our peace?" (Cf. 2 Kings 7:1-20)

4. Comment on the kind of church that produces evangelists like Philip and Stephen.

5. Where would an evangelist go to find a pulpit in Jerusalem?

6. Name some true evangelists in the church today. Do you know a church permeated with "every-member evangelism"?

FOOTNOTES

1 Hebrews 5:12, TSB
2 Titus 1:5-9; 1 Tim. 3:1-7
3 Isaiah 52:7; Rom. 10:15
4 Jeremiah 20:9
5 Rom. 10:16-21; Isa. 53:1; Psa. 19:4; Isa. 65:1-2
6 2 Kings 7:1-20
7 Acts 6:3
8 Acts 8:4
9 Eph. 4:11
10 Matt. 28:18-20; Mark 16:16; Luke 24:45-48
11 Acts 6:1-7
12 Eph. 4:11-12
13 Confer Everett Ferguson, "The Ministry of the Word In The First Two Centuries," *Restoration Quarterly*, 1957, p. 23; and Geoffrey Ellis, "The Evangelist," *Christian Teaching*, 1981, pp. 197-207.

[14] Mark 1:14-15
[15] Acts 8:4; 11:19
[16] Mark 16:15-16
[17] Ibid, p. 203-204
[18] Gal. 6:7; 2 Cor. 9:6
[19] Luke 8
[20] 1 Peter 3:15
[21] 1 Cor. 11:26
[22] Acts 14:27
[23] Tex Williams gives a most eloquent and thorough view of the hardships encountered by missionaries who endeavor to find support for entering the foreign fields of labor, on cassette recording, "Jesus, the Hope of a Materialistic World," 1980, available from Star Bible, Fort Worth. Williams, Director of Sunset School of Missions, has traveled world-wide and speaks from experience and first hand knowledge.

How Christianity
Is Growing In
The City of Boston 16

Frequently someone asks, "Are these first century methods being tried anywhere today? Will it work in our generation and in our culture?" A "model" (1 Thess. 1:6-7) may be seen at least in many aspects as we hear in this chapter an exciting story of faith, courage, freedom and victory.

Boston is the capital of Massachusetts and the largest city in New England. It is a major manufacturing center, a great seaport, a center of education, arts, and scientific research. Boston is renowned as "The Cradle of Liberty" because it led American colonists in their struggle for independence from Great Britain. The town began in the 1630's when a preacher named William Blackstone settled there with other "Puritans" searching for religious freedom.

Boston's population grew to 24,000 by the time of the Revolutionary War in 1776. Today the metropolitan area has four million lost souls.

The city ranks next to Chicago as the second largest Roman Catholic archdiocese in the United States. The "Unitarian Universalist Association" and the "Church of Christ, Scientists" have headquarters here. Some of the world's renowned educational institutions are located here, many of which were founded by devoutly religious people. Today, hundreds of church buildings may be seen throughout the city, dating back to the 1700's; Old North Church, built in 1723, is the oldest.

The struggles of men who endeavored to re-establish the practices of early Christians date back in a real sense to the 1500's with the Puritans in England. Robert Browne (cir. 1550-1633) was one of their early leaders. They later settled in Plymouth and Boston in the New World. Their aim was to purify the churches of priestly vestments and elaborate ceremonies imposed upon them by the powerful clergy. Some wanted to do away with church music, statues and colored windows in church houses. They thought each church should be independent of all others and free to choose its own "pastor." They thought any member had the right to preach. Many who settled in the Boston area gave their lives in valiant efforts to provide an environment of freedom from religious tyranny for themselves and their children. Though they aspired to take the Bible only as a guide, they were encumbered by Calvin's doctrine and by certain traditions of their own. Unfortunately, they later developed a spirit of intolerance that disallowed religious liberty to others who did not share their views. They raised up a small but formidable militia and frequently hanged intruders that infiltrated their settlements.

Today, the influence of the Puritans is still widely felt in a large segment of Protestantism, though their existence as a distinct body came to an end in 1660 with the return of the Stuart dynasty.

The Lexington Church — Story of Struggles

The earliest efforts among the current restoration

leaders to plant a continuing church in this area did not emerge until 1921 in Brookline. This and a few other small congregations were assisted by young men who had come to further their educations at Harvard, M.I.T., Boston University, or one of the other 200 colleges and Universities of the city. The Lexington congregation was formed in 1956, then Melrose followed. Burlington started with a bang in 1967 when Don Humphrey led an impressive "Exodus" of southern families to this Boston suburb. These and a few other congregations have assembled through these years, but none had ever experienced what could be considered a rapid addition to their numbers, much less "daily" additions or "multiplication" of disciples as we read in the book of Acts. That is, not until 1979 when God began speaking through a "small cloud" of witnesses, about the size of a man's hand.

The Boston Church — Story of Faith and Victory

Here is how it began. The forces of the Lexington church, like some of the others in the greater Boston area, were discouraged through a decade of declining attendance and, in fact, dissolution was seriously considered by the little band of about forty souls. Various methods and men had come and gone, and some had concluded that New England was simply an unfruitful field, especially elite Boston with its myriad of sophisticated cultures.

There was a young man 25 years of age by the name of Kip McKean who had been experiencing a degree of success as a campus minister in another state. He had heard of the languishing condition of the Lexington church, and was asked to come and help. When he began to seriously consider the move, his friends cautioned him of endangering his reputation through what would probably turn out to be another slow or even further declining ministry in this field already proven to be extremely difficult. But he came, hoping against hope that God could work through these obstacles if his own faith could become strong enough. If his courage and vision could by God's grace be made to grow through the trials and hardships that would await him, perhaps in time God would show that He has "many people in this city."

And so he came, along with his wife Elena and about ten young people, the first week in June, 1979. He already knew that he could not accomplish anything by his own strength, but trusted that God's power could do more than he could imagine as it would work in him and in the few Christians at Lexington (Eph. 3:20). Kip began to instill his own vision into the hearts of the rest, of how God's power could work through all of them if each one would accept the challenge of teaching and training others to teach in the spirit of 2 Timothy 2:2: "The things that thou hast heard from me among many witnesses, the same commit thou to faithful men who shall be able to teach others also." With this new spark of enthusiastic ledership the people had a mind to work and set about to train themselves to do the work of discipling their neighbors, friends and relatives. Three weeks after arriving, 170 people came to a "Bring Your Neighbor Day" just about filling the little meeting house at Lexington. Evangelistic Bible studies were begun in a few homes during the week. With practically every member participating in these evangelistic "Bible talks", God began fulfilling promises He had made to those who sow the seed bountifully. By the end of the first year, 103 had been immersed into Christ. The work of sowing and reaping continued into the second year, adding more Bible talks not only in homes but also in some offices and dormitory rooms. By the end of the second year, God had given further increase by adding 200 more.

By this time, elders Paul McNeal, Bob Gempel and Russell Hulbert were looking around for additional space for the Lord's Day assemblies. A Baptist church house was rented in 1980 in nearby Arlington that would seat 550, and the services began at 11:30 after the Baptists had worshipped and vacated. This was soon filled to overflowing, forcing the brethren to seek professional help from the real estate brokers to locate other facilites. The third year 256 more were baptized. Bob Gempel gave up his occupation to enter full time shepherding. Steve Johnson, Doug Arthur, Jim Lloyd, Doug Blough and then Frank Kim were added as evangelists to help Kip McKean in the work of evangelizing and discipling, having been baptized and discipled to Christ for years by him before being appointed evangelists. 368 were baptized the fourth year and approximately 90% remaining faithful. By the end of the fourth year, God was adding more than a soul daily, as was done in Jerusalem in century one (Acts 2:47). The fifth year of the work saw 457, and now well into their sixth year of "making disciples" it seems certain they will baptize well over 600! Contributions increased from $250 weekly in 5½ years to $25,000.

As they continued in their search, strangely and yet perhaps providentially, not only one, but TWO church buildings *burned,* one during negotiations and another just after a purchase contract was signed. With assemblies now being conducted in a High School auditorium and at the nearby Baptist building simultaneously, the leadership hired professional scouts to find a place to either rent or buy that would accomodate the growing crowd. God soon led them to the ornate and famous Boston Opera House on Washington Street in downtown Boston. The elders leased this magnificant 2600-seat facility for a three year term, assuming that even this will become inadequate for the ever increasing 1800 member congregation which attends regularly (February, 1985).

With the outreach extending throughout the metropolis, the name on the church bulletin was changed from Lexington to Boston church of Christ. The 1983 bulletins listed over 125 evangelistic Bible talks each week, but this number a year later exceeded 190.

Each Christian is expected to participate in one of these talks each week by (1) being present and (2) by inviting visitors to come. By applying the every-member evangelism method as was recorded in Acts 8:4, they expect to see a multiplying effect that will "fill all the city" with the gospel teaching within a few years.

Discipleship Partners

For many years this congregation has employed a method for building stronger relationships between two Christians. Essentially, this found its Biblical basis in the "one another" passages such as John 13:34-35, Galatians 5:13, Hebrews 3:12-13 and many, many others. There is no question, these relationships have greatly helped to keep people faithful after being baptized, and have served as a great forum for discipling each other to Christ.

(1.) **Bible Study**: Just how the hour or two of discipleship partners begins each week will differ, but sometime during this time a primary focus will be a study in God's Word.

(2.) **Life Discussion**: Flowing quite naturally from weekly Scripture study based on need, would be a discussion on how to practically apply these Biblical principles.

(3.) **Prayers**: The greatest untapped source of power in the world today is prayer (Ephesians 1:18-20). Having studied the Scriptures to understand God's specific will in the Christian's area of need then having received counseling on the unique aspects of each situation,

140

prayer is needed for God to help us.

The concept of Discipleship Partners is modeled on the relationship that Jesus had with the Twelve as well as the relationships between the disciples (Mathew 28: 19).[1]

Elders, Evangelist, Deacons and other trusted teachers lead in 31 "house churches" (Philemon 2) throughout the metropolis under the supervision of the elders. They meet regularly in these groups with 50 or more members in each. Evangelist Kip McKean wrote in January, 1984, about the beginning of a Spanish language house church and gives some insight into his vision of the structure of the city-wide community of believers under one leadership. Here are his words:

> "The Protestant model of a small church building with a steeple, holding a couple hundred people of one language for a worship service does not meet the needs of metropolitian evangelism. The pattern of the giant New Testament churches was to meet all together in one place if possible (Acts 2:41,44). However, many times this simply was not feasible given the large distances involved in the city and because of the death-threatening persecution. Therefore the Christians often met in small units called house churches (Romans 16:5, Philemon 2, Acts 8:3). The Bible pattern is abundantly clear that there was always one eldership in one city (Acts 15:2, Acts 20:17, Philippians 1:1). These God ordained men (Acts 20:28) were in authority over the different meetings of the one church in that city. In Boston, we foresee a day when other languages such as French and Chinese will serve as the com-

Diagram of Boston Church Assemblies

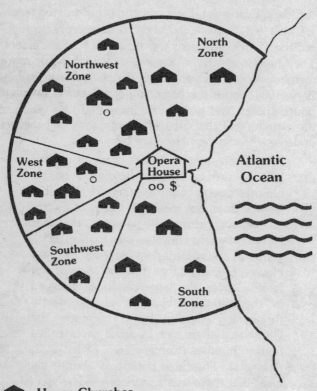

House Churches
o **Elders**
$ **Treasury**

Diagram #10

[Compare with Jerusalem church on page 51.]

mon element for other house churches within the Boston congregation. Thus we hope to gently challenge those whose Protestant thinking is so dominant in our society; the challenge is simply to return to the scriptures and truly restore the New Testament patterns of worship."

—Bulletin, January 29, 1984

The approach toward the goal of **one church** in Boston as seen above was earlier expressed by McKean in a personal letter to the author of this book in its first edition, June 24, 1983:

"We have been using your book, 3 R's of Urban Church Growth", as a topic for discussion in the elders and deacons discipleship group on Sunday mornings before church. All of us have marvelled at the similarity of ideas that we have gleaned from God's Word. We appreciate your scholarship and your practical thinking as it has challenged us to drive even farther into the text of God's Word searching for the patterns and parallels in the New Testament church of the first century."[1]

The Boston church is by no ways and means the only church in the Boston area. However, though to the pragmatist a seeming impossibility, the elders dream of a day when all churches in the Boston world unite on God's Word and give a unified witness to a lost world.

A World Vision

But to the elders (2), evangelists (8), and deacons (9), the field is not only Boston's **four million,** but the world's **four billion.** Mission teams have been trained and sent to London, New York City and Chicago where hundreds have already obeyed Jesus Christ in response to these three ministries trained at the Boston church. A dozen "intern"families are now in training with their eyes on Paris, Washingtion, D.C., Tokyo, Philadelphia, Rio de Janiero, Bombay and fifteen other major cities of the world. In October of 1983 and again in October of 1984 a cash contribution of about $300,000 was taken for world missions, not counting an additional $100,000 in pledges to support various mission teams. It is truly convicting to realize that 90% of those who gave have been Christians less than 5 years. What a great spirit of excitement pervaded the Opera House when 2,500 participants in the church's World Missions Seminar heard scores of vibrant messages from God's men who are seasoned foreign missionaries and from those who are planning to "go into all the world and preach the gospel to every creature"! They are striving for members to either "plan to go" or "stay to grow".

Dr. Jerry Jones, evangelist and former Chairman of the Bible Department at Harding University, has recently moved with his family to work with the Boston church. And so has Dr. George Gurganus, former Director of Missions, Abilene Christian University. Clinton Brazle and Ken Erb are just two among several who have formerly served with distinction as ministers and/or elders who have moved to Boston to train with teams targeting great urban centers. Jerry Jones wrapped up his report of the 1984 missions seminar in these exciting words:

> "The closing part of the seminar left one question in the minds of all: Where do we go from here? The answer is clear — into all the world. The world that needs the gospel begins in our neighborhoods and on our jobs. The world is literally at our doors needing the gospel. This seminar left everyone with the attitude of

'Lord, here am I, send me!' By God's grace
and relying upon His strength, the Seminar
convinced all that our generation will see
the gospel taken to the whole world, barring
the coming of Jesus."

To you in Boston, we say, as Paul did when writing
the church in Thessalonica, "You became a model to all
the believers . . . your faith in God has become known
everywhere" (1 Thess. 1:6-8).

God has proved His Word again in this "hardest mission field of the U.S.A." Who among us ten years ago,
even five years ago, could have thought or imagined that
such victories could have been wrought? God continues
to "do immeasurably more than all we ask or imagine
according to his power that is at work within us, to him
be glory in the church and in Christ Jesus throughout
all generations, for ever and ever! Amen."

(Eph 3:20-21, NIV)

QUESTIONS

1. Does the Bible hold up any local church as an "example"
   or "model"?
2. What year did Kip McKean begin his ministry in Boston?
   Did his friends encourage him to go to this city?
3. Can you name the three cities to which the Boston church
   has sent teams of evangelistic workers?
4. What scriptures justify the "discipleship partners" for building stronger relationships between Christians?
5. Describe the "house church" arrangement in Boston and
   how all of them are coordinated under one eldership in
   the city.
6. How does Jerry Jones answer the question, "Where do
   we go from here?"

FOOTNOTES

1 Kip McKean, Bulletin, April 22, 1984.

2 How grossly mistaken has one prophet of doom proved to be. He wrote in 1981: "A disorderly, disjointed structure such as house churches all under a single eldership would in our day and time destroy the church and drive it underground."

3 For a further report on the widely divergent acceptance/rejection of the elders' scope of oversight and the city church set forth in *3 R's of Urban Church Growth*, see the Epilogue. The organizational structure of the Boston church is shown here:

1. The Elders oversee the entire church.
2. Evangelists appointed by the elders administer each of the five zones. The Evangelist is to disciple the House Church leaders and and help them with difficult situations in each house church.
3. The House church leaders are to disciple the people in their house church and make sure their physical, emotional, and spiritual needs are being met.
4. Within each house church, weekly evangelistic Bible talks are organized. Each house has 3 - 10 of these Bible talks. Each member participates in just one.
5. When the zone, house church & Bible talk grows to a certain size it divides. Thus, because growth and division takes place at all levels multiplication is the result.

(Letter from Kip McKean, February 18, 1985)

[*Postscript*. The Boston church recently had over 2800 in an assembly at the Boston Gardens. With membership doubling every 18 months, within a few years they may not be able to have all the church together in one place each Lord's Day. This author, in talking with a Boston elder about this possibility while standing in the foyer of the Opera House in 1983, observed that if meetings every week had to be conducted in many houses or places, it would be that much nearer to the practice of the first century urban churches.]

How To Begin

If the *readin, ritin and rithmetic* of these chapters seem accurate in principle to the reader, after making a thorough examination through study and prayer, he may want an opinion as to how the concept can be put before the brethren of his city. Seeing the truths and the benefits is one step; knowing how to proceed wisely and harmlessly[1] is the next.

Presentation To Leaders

Most urban church leaders meet together occasionally for fellowship meals at which studies or programs of common interest are presented. This affords an ideal setting where the concepts can be shown with feedback and discussion from the group. This will open up other opportunities for presentations before similar groups in other communities to elderships or even before entire congregations of the area.[2]

35mm slides are available which can be projected during the discourse. They will help to keep the thinking together and will clarify as the charts and diagrams of the book are shown. (These 40 slides are available with a cassette narration from Star Bible, catalog #2003S.) A blackboard is also effective.

Distributing copies of the book will help as a guide to personal Bible study and confirmation of the plan. A chapter by chapter study in class or group situations

147

would be beneficial, especially if the thought questions at the end of each chapter are discussed.

Seek Sponsorship

In order to attain harmony among the congregations and a favorable acceptance of these biblical procedures, sponsorship by an existing eldership would be advantageous where congregations already exist in the city. It would be simple upon natural evangelistic impulse to go ahead without such an endorsement by an existing congregation, especially when a family or families are already offering their home as a place of assembly. Out of respect for the brethren who may not understand your motives and who may not have had opportunity to study these things through, we would recommend that this impulse be restrained for a reasonable length of time. Patience and prayer should at God's proper time enable you to proceed with their fellowship and moral encouragement. You do not want to create a division and be branded "anti-building" and destroy your opportunity to help bring about a greater unity and evangelistic thrust among all the brethren of the city than they have ever enjoyed. Remember your goal is greater harmony, love and productivity to the glory of God.

It is possible and may be expected in some cities that more than one eldership or even all elderships may jointly launch the plan. That would be wonderful indeed and would greatly accelerate realization of the goal of city-wide and world-wide evangelism.

The eldership(s) could consider adoption of a foundation plan such as the following:

1. Agree to sponsor one or more home assemblies conducted on Lord's days by trusted teacher(s).
2. Offer direction and encouragement to assure the successful growth and biblical faithfulness of the group(s).
3. Adopt a plan of supporting the teaching, preaching

and shepherding of the house assembly, by the assembly, so as to increase the ministry force.

4. Consider adopting additional features as time progresses that will keep pace with the rapid city-wide growth, such as a name that would suggest a city-wide church.

Advertising

Other congregations can be invited to participate by invitation through the mail, by phone or by personal contact. A letter designed to be sent to out-of-duty members or those known to be "unused" where they are (especially former preachers and leaders) has been drafted and appears in the appendix. Also a proposed wording for a brochure appears in the appendix containing a listing of benefits obtainable through this assembly approach.

To generate interest among those outside the body of Christ, any and all honorable and effective means may be employed including:

1. Contact friends, relatives, neighbors.
2. Door to door canvassing.
3. Telephone contact.
4. Distribution of gospel literature.
5. Newspaper advertising.
6. Radio and TV programs.
7. Publicizing the public meetings.
8. Contacts made through benevolent, hospital, jail, or marketplace ministries..

New Views?

Some have asked, "what are the new views you are advocating?" These are not new but are so unused, they appear to be new. They reach back beyond the Restoration Movement of the nineteenth century, all the way back to the church in Jerusalem. In an effort to restore Christianity in its original truth and purity, there is an inclination to stop short on our way with the great truths

149

discovered by the great pioneers of the American frontier who were finding their way out of the maze of denominational error. Men like Barton W. Stone, Alexander Campbell, Walter Scott, Jacob Creath and others fought through a jungle of traditions and delivered to a grateful host of their day an appeal to turn away from following the clergy with their creeds and catechisms. They urged men to go all the way back past Protestantism and past Rome to the old Jerusalem gospel.

Diagram #11

BACK TO JERUSALEM

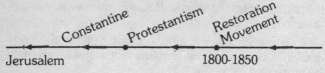

Jerusalem   1800-1850

Their work was amazingly effective and thousands heeded the call of Jesus through their tongues and pens. Later generations may read of their works and how God blessed them and gave increase. However, it has long been recognized that a weakness, or as Paul said, "a wrong" was committed by some of the wealthy preachers who in their opposition to the "hireling clergy " went to the opposite extreme of not accepting any financial support for their labors. While they were able to support themselves from the wealth of farms and herds, other evangelists, in not so favorable a circumstance, were hindered from entering the ministry. Because Campbell and a few other independently wealthy men had refused pay, in many cases the brethren concluded that *no man who preaches should receive pay.* This one defect reminds us that it is unlikely that any man or movement has completely restored the true New Testament church in all its aspects.

Others have asked, "How will elders keep control if there are groups meeting under their oversight away from the church building?" I see no reason for losing control of what is taught or done in a home when the teacher or evangelist is known to be faithful and when he is properly supervised by elders of the church. If they could trust him in a foreign country to preach, surely they can trust him in their own city.

Conclusion

The basic positions of this book are established if one church can have (1) *different assembly places* so as to accommodate the deaf or language groups or because of limitation of meeting facilities; or (2) *different assembly times* because of limitation of space such as in early and late Sunday services, or because of convenience for members who can more easily assemble at one hour than another.[2]

Our aim and heart's desire is expressed by inspiration in Ephesians 3:20-21

> "Now unto him that is able to do exceedingly abundantly above all that we ask or think, according to the power that worketh in us, unto him be the glory in the church and in Christ Jesus unto all generations for ever and ever. Amen."

QUESTIONS

1. What are some groups to whom this plan can be presented in your area?

2. What tools are available for the presentation?

3. Why is sponsorship necessary?

4. Discuss the time element and the dangers of haste.

5. What are some of the first steps to be taken by the sponsoring church(es)?

FOOTNOTES

[1] Matthew 10:16

[2] Please refer to chapter 8 "When Ye Come Together" for a fuller discussion of the principles of this paragraph.

EPILOGUE

I welcome this opportunity to correct some typographical errors in this book's first edition *(3 R's of Urban Church Growth)*, to provide a report on responses to it, and to give more information that will be pertinent. Interest in the propositions advanced by me some four years ago has increased to such an extent that it is possible in this brief epilogue to provide only a survey of what has transpired.

Since attention can be drawn to only a few of the responses to the first edition, we shall limit our remarks to those which can be expected to have some influence or to evoke reaction in future discussion. We shall notice this response in the following sequence:

Forum Discussions
Negative Response
Positive Response

Forum Discussion

Hardeman Nichols, moderating in an open forum at the Fort Worth Lectures in January of 1982, just a few months after the 3 R's books had appeared, led a discussion in some sensitive areas introduced in the book. One question from the audience that generated a lengthy discussion was, "Is the 3 R's book by Alvin Jennings Scriptural?" Nichols responded that the "whole church" meeting together represents an "ideal" but said Paul knew exceptions would occur such as the sick, travelers, etc.

He further stated it would "not be unscriptural to have several groups meeting at different places in the same building . . . English, Spanish, etc. It is not sinful to do so. If you have a large number and cannot take care of them in one place, why not have another assembly?" In reference to Acts 5:25 he asked, "How many congregations were there in Jerusalem? I think you'd say 'one', as Curtis Porter often referred to Acts 5:23-25 where the apostles (plural) were praying and standing and teaching — all at the same time but not to the same audience." Was it necessary to make different autonomous congregations where the apostles were dealing with different groups? Was it mandatory that the 3,000 (Acts 2:42) continue steadfastly in the Lord's Supper all in one single assembly? Hugo McCord at the same session concurred that all are *not* required to assemble at the same time and place in order to be a church; he disagreed when L.M. contended the Lord's Supper must not be served outside the one assembly "all together." Nichols said, "I have never been in a large church when *all* were present — some buildings will not hold them all at one place, shift-workers cannot all come at the same time, etc. Don't make laws where God made none! How can you cram 1800 into an auditorium of only 1,000 seats?" This discussion, tape recorded, also carried these poignant questions? "If one eldership oversees two groups in one building, why not oversee all assemblies in a city?" Such immature assertions as these were also made: "Even if there are three different language groups all meeting in one building, they must be three separate congregations — not under one eldership!" (G.W., Texas). Again, "We would not think of having the Lord's Supper in 2 or 3 assemblies" (G.E., Tennessee).

James P. Needham, editor of *Torch,* wrote in February, 1982 concerning the liberties in assembling that "a church can scripturally offer the Supper to fewer than the whole assembly." Again, it is a "false assumption that

Troas had only one assembly." . . . "The language would be the same if they had come together 10 times to break bread, it could still be said, 'and on the first day of the week when the disciples came together to break bread.' . . . We must be very careful not to read between the lines the things that are not there but which in our traditional practice and beliefs we wish were there." (pages 4,8,10).

Prohibiton of Meetings In Private Houses?

Reports have been circulated about alleged prohibitions against Bible studies and/or worship gatherings in private homes in Los Angeles and other cities. Tom Bradley, Mayor of Los Angeles, writing in a personal letter to the author on Feb. 24, 1983, says: "This is absolutely false . . . There is not now, nor has there ever been a prohibition against Bible studies in Los Angeles." He did speak of an opinion issued by a Deputy City Attorney in 1980 based on "inaccurate assumptions". The mayor did make reference to a statement by the Department of Building and Safety which prohibited meetings in a private residence whether religious or not, that consisted of loud speaking or music which disturbs the neighbors.

A similar prohibition reportedly prevailed in the city of Baltimore, also denied by the Baltimore City Law Department in a personal letter to the author, April 18, 1983. ". . . church services are permitted in all residential zoning districts."

There has been no evidence presented contrary to these herein given.

Negative Response
(A) G.K.W.

Although response has been overwhelmingly positive, I feel obligated to clarify my position since it has been misconstrued by a few. I am especially surprised at the comments by G.K.W. of Florida. Several have written as did John Mark Hicks of Alexandria, Virginia: "I was saddened by G.K. W.'s article concerning your book. I felt he misrepresented you and did not understand what your proposal is. I regret that this brother has publicly misrepresented your workable and excellent proposals." Among other things, in his review of my book he stated, "It is also taught in the book that congregational autonomy should fade (p. 56)." (Gospel Advocate, Nov. 19, 1981, p. 681). To have misquoted what I wrote on this point is most unfortunate. I regret that he did not *correctly* quote: "Congregational autonomy will begin to fade WITHIN THE CITY." By distorting this vital statement, he proceeded to demonstrate our complete abandonment of the principle of independence of the church in each city from the church in every other city. Having done this, he then accuses me of advocating a corrupted organization like the hierarchy of Roman Catholicism. Once he abused my statement, he then drew many erroneous conclusions about a 'diocese', 'metro elders' over 'congregational elders' over a 'one-man pastor' system meeting in a home, etc. The review fails to recognize that our view is that there is only one eldership in each city, and no group of "super" elders are over any other elders. All the elders in the city supervise all the church in that city, even though obviously an elder will be more intimately concerned about those with whom he meets more frequently. I do believe, as stated on numerous occasions, in the complete autonomy of the local church; however, I do not believe the local church in the New Testament era was necessarily confined to the four walls of any building. This is one of the traditional notions handed down from which I hope all can escape who are not blinded by pharisaic tradition or prejudice.

The article referenced above expressed other concerns too numerous to itemize here. His employment of what I consider to be unethical polemical tactics left the impression with me (and others) that he was more bent on destroying his opponent than in arriving at the truth on the matters at hand. So different are the positions he feels he has perceived in the book to what it actually states that his review led one preacher to ask, "Could I see a copy of your NEW REVISED EDITION of the 3 R's book? I read your first edition three times and have never found in it what the reviewer saw." I replied that there had been no revised edition.

(B) P.C.

Another reviewer of *3 R's of Urban Church Growth* prophesied the doom of any who dared implement the principles therein. Writing in March, 1981, before the phenomenally successful labors with house churches in America became an historic fact, P.C. of Texas wrote: "A disorderly, disjointed structure such as house churches all under a single eldership would in our day and time destroy the church and drive it underground." I recommend (1) that he look again at the New Testament, and at (2) the Boson church as described in a new chapter in this book. Jeremiah's words concerning prophets whose message comes not to pass would seem to be appropriate (Jer. 29:9; 23:16).

(C) H.J.

Another reviewer, H.J. of Texas, predicted in 1981 the issuance of *3 R's of Urban Church Growth* would ruin the author's reputation as a gospel preacher and bring about the destruction of Star Bible Publications of which he is the founder and president. He said that the book contains "the most dangerous heresy ever put before the brotherhood." To these three predictions, I can only respond that (1) if speaking what I believe to be the truth in love destroys my reputation as a preacher, then I must be willing to accept that consequence in the light of 2 Tim. 3:12. (2) Star Bible has enjoyed a steady growth and by God's grace is now experiencing the best years of its 20-year history. (3) God will judge righteously as to which is "the most dangerous of all heresies." We shall continue to pray that our critics favor us with specific biblical corrections so that we might be able to see clearly our faults. This reviewer made no *specific* accusation.

(D) E.W.

An elder, also director of a preacher training school described his reaction as *"violent"* and wrote in a letter Feb. 10, 1981: "The methods that you have outlined in your book are the first steps to a religious hierarchical system similar to the embryo of Roman Catholicism. It is cultic to the core. This book will ruin you in the brotherhood. I will oppose this effort in every way that is open to me." And he has.

(E) Eldership

The elders of the local church where my wife and I were members asked me to teach the main adult class, on the condition that the 3 R's book be removed from the market and "let it die a natural death" (May 19, 1982). Although my love for them was genuine, to concede to them would have seemed as a compromising or hushing of truths that needed to be heard. We did not stop the book, so became mute in all the public preaching and teaching at that place from that day on.

(F) Star Board Members

Publication of the 3 R's book set in motion opposition particularly on the part of two personal friends who were members of the Star Board of Directors. When I refused to withdraw the book from publication as they demanded, they either resigned so as to escape any identification with it, or were asked to resign to eliminate continuing disruption at the board meetings. One of these brothers has persisted in his campaign to denounce the book, and has publicly disavowed fellowship with me. Feeling these pressures, one by one other board members either resigned or quietly dropped out, reducing the number from twelve to only three. Most of these men either elders, preachers or deacons in nearby congregations, had all been chosen from among my most admired personal friends.

Needless to say, these events involving close personal friends of long standing hurt very deeply. Were it not for the faith we had in God and His Word, coupled with the abundance of encouragement from many others who spoke and wrote positively as will be seen below, we would have despaired and lost hope.

Positive Response

The most convincing evidence that any Christian author could expect is that he has written a book that has been accepted. At this writing, the first edition has been completely sold out. At the time of writing in 1980, I simply took the New Testament and from it wrote down what appeared recorded there, with a deliberate attempt to divorce myself from 20th century ecclesiastical practices. I tried to be objective and fair with God's Word as well as with all persons and practices involved, praying that no truth would be withheld for fear it might meet with an unpleasant consequence. I then believed as I now believe, that the "search for truth is the noblest occupation of man; its publication a duty" as quoted from the words of Madame Stael, and printed in our introductory pages. While the negative responses have been painful as predicted and as expected, still they have been relatively few and for the most part, I feel, are due to a failure of my readers to clearly conceive the concepts we were striving to communicate. While my own weakness in ability of expression through writing has doubtless contributed to this failure, at the same time I am convinced that the major problem has been that traditional practices have become so deeply imbedded that some readers have been blinded to what I have actually stated. They have not allowed themselves to see, lest the changes consequent upon their acknowledgment be judged as disruptive and consequently unhappy.

While hundreds of letters of commendation have been received, less than a dozen could be counted as negative. To balance or offset the above critical responses, a few of the letters of appreciation are given below.

"I accept as biblical your idea that there can be elders over a metroplex church. I think that is clear from Titus 1:5 and Acts 14:23."

(J.M.H., Virginia, May 15, 1981)

"Alvin, when you are right, and know you are right, and can biblically prove it, don't back down. G.K. Wallace is not the standard."

(K.H., Texas, Feb. 6, 1982)

"After reading your "3 R's of Urban Church Growth" I am glad to learn there is at least one other person who believes and thinks as I do. . . . .

I don't believe there is even a small chance of any elders sponsoring a home assembly program. They have gone too far into building programs and leading the flock to economic slaughter. Our home is in _____ and we have been members of the ___ congregation. They recently moved into a 2 million dollar building. They are saddling each member with a built in debt of $2,000 each plus interest and overhead of some $500,000 per year. A family of five would cost some $10,000 to "join" plus another $1,000 per year to keep the facility going."

(C.M.H., Texas, Aug. 1, 1981)

"About three years ago I held a position which stated we must withdraw from churches that have multiple assemblies. I began to see inconsistencies in the position and turned from it. . . . We try too hard to squeeze the NT into our American, western concepts. We are no different from the Baptist, etc., when we do so."

(R.H., Tennessee, May 26, 1981)

"I have just finished reading your book "3R's of Urban Church Growth" and I must say it is certainly different from the present system used by churches of Christ today. I agree with most of what you say, but my dear Bro. you and I will probably be a long time gone from this earth before these ideas are put into practice. You are a voice crying in the wilderness. You will encounter much opposition to this system you advocate. The reason being in my opinion, that the average church member today has simply stopped working in the kingdom; he has hired someone to do his work for him.

The plan we use today has taken approx. 100 yrs. to mature and we finally reached the point of no "church growth" — It had to come. As an elder in the church I am very well acquainted with some of the problems you talk about.

I must admire you for at least trying — I was surprised we still had men who even thought along these lines."

(M.R., Virginia, March 8, 1981)

"In my opinion Mr. Wallace got his remarks mixed up. It should have been that false doctrines of Catholicism, Baptists, Jehovah's Witnesses and others have crept into the Lord's church and not your book.

Your book is simply trying to get believers to follow the New Testament Pattern instead of the Baptist and Denominational Pattern.

This outburst by Mr. Wallace proves once again that many in the Lord's church are as radical as the Catholics and pagan rulers in the first century. If you say anything contrary to their traditions, they will throw you to the lions."

(C.M.H., Texas, Jan. 18, 1982)

"Terry Blake just bequeathed your new book "3 R's of Urban Church Growth" and I must say it was challenging. You will get a lot of flack, but I must say that I have felt what you have written for a long time . . . so has Terry. I'm glad somebody took the time to write it down.

Elders in every city? Sure. Not a plurality in every little group that meets. I've always felt that way. It can work. It did work. It won't work unless we open our eyes. I hope your book will help us to see a little better. Bless you for it."

(S.C.G., Michigan, April 15, 1981)

"Terry Blake just returned from the Soul-Winning Workshop in Tulsa all excited about a book by Alvin Jennings. For years Alvin has been one of my most admired church leaders and thinkers and his new book "3 R's of Urban Church Growth" only confirms my feelings about him. You can order it from Star for $1.95. It will change your perspective about our mission to reach out to the lost. We are slipping behind every day. Like Alice in Wonderland, we must run as fast as we can to stay right where we are. This book will change your attitude about evangelism for the better. Alvin has done more than any man I know to get the word into the homes of every American via the printed page."

(Bulletin article, Michigan, Apr. 19, 1981)

"We have been using your book *3 R's of Urban Church Growth* as a topic for discussion in the elders and deacons discipleship group on Sunday mornings before church. All of us have marvelled at the similarity of ideas that we have gleaned from Gods' word. We appreciate your scholarship and your practical thinking as it has challenged us to drive even farther into the text of God's word searching for the patterns and parallels in the New Testament church of the first century."

(K.M., Massachusetts, June 24, 1983)

"Concerning your new book — you have said some things that needed to be said a long time ago. The traditionalism and institutionalism prevalent in many of our churches today thwarts their growth and will eventually kill them unless a reversal is seen. I think that you have done a great deal to point us in the right direction."

(D.S.F., Pennsylvania, April 23, 1981)

"Basically, I agree with your argument and have wanted for years to see this type of approach used here in our great city. Up to now, however, I've met with no success in trying to convince the majority of my co-workers of its potential."

(G.S., Brazil, July 8, 1981)

"I am extremely excited about the concepts presented in the *Three R's of Urban Church Growth!* I have felt this way for a long time. There is a town where I plan to set up a "pilot model" to see if the methods will work in the field. The date planned is June 1, 1989 (5 years)."

(D.B.W., Arkansas, July 14, 1983)

"I think that there are some places (especially in new works) where some of your ideas are being carried out. Of course, we as a whole are pretty much bound by tradition. . . . If we can get just a few brethren to break over and try some new ideas for soul winning, and be successful, then perhaps others will be encouraged to follow."

(J.T.B., Oregon, Feb. 16, 1984)

"Also I wish to thank you for introducing me to your *3 R's* book. It has also been helpful to our mission strategy. Both elders here at _____ have read it now and have told me it has opened their eyes. They are determined to start making changes, and lead the church back to the Bible and Living Like Christ. . . . We were very impressed by the content of your little booklet; so were our elders."

(T.E., Texas, March 4, 1984)

"I believe your book on the *3 R's* could be a gospel bomb if it was followed."

(D.D., Missouri, Mar. 23, 1984)

". . . concerning information on organizing house churches. I am very interested in this concept, finding it very biblical (more biblical?) than many current practices. Thanks for your leadership and example of Christlikeness."

(E.D., Oklahoma, April 4, 1984)

"Alvin, so far as I can see your biggest crime in writing such a book as this (though I have not read it yet) is that you are thinking for yourself. You are not following along in the footsteps of brotherhood tradition and you are not afraid to think new thoughts for yourself and then to let people know what you are thinking. But you must surely know by now that when you question traditional brotherhood thinking, you are on extremely dangerous ground and you can expect to be persecuted from all sides. When you question traditional concepts and practices, it frightens brethren who have never thought for themselves . . . I appreciate you also for thinking independently and being brave enough to tell what you believe. The brethren may curse you but I believe the Lord will bless you."

(D.S., April 6, 1981)

"I have read your "3 R's" book from cover to cover very carefully and want you to know that I think it is an excellent treatise. I am not agreeing with you just for the sake of agreement, but those of us who have been on the mission field for as long as we have couldn't agree with you more. For 16 years we have been trying to do *just exactly* what you propose in this book, and may I say, with success. I do not know much about "Crossroadsim", but I do know that your ideas work beautifully and scripturally in the nation of Guatemala. We have tried to establish a 1st-Century concept (as near as possible) in the churches of that great city in Guatemala, Guatemala City. We've stood on our heads to help make those 15 churches as autonomous, as self-governing, self-sustaining and self-propagating as we could. I do think, however, that your proposals are perhaps ahead of their time even though you have so logically attempted to show our brotherhood the necessity of going *back* 2,000 years. Your book will come into its own. We've (in my opinion) become so saturated in our thinking that for a church to be great and render great service to the kingdom it must, of necessity, be large. Those of us who have been on the mission field know better. If you need a voice that would support you in your proposals, I am convinced that I can add mine. I can find *nothing* in your book that has not been carefully

164

researched and documented. It is as scriptural as it needs to be, and frankly, I think you did a *great* job! I think that this thing of 1,2,3, & 5 millions of dollars saddled around the necks of our brethren in building huge monuments *to ourselves* is all backwards, Bro. Jennings. This is vanity of men. That kind of thing does NOT get the precious word out to the ones who need it. I agree 100% with Bro. Woodward that, "our big beautiful buildings have become a detriment to (our) elderships." To a missionary who really knows church growth methods, don't talk to him about building buildings for natives on the field . . . your conversation will fall on deaf ears. On the other hand, if the missionary is looking for a monument to be built to himself, he will listen attentatively.

On page 84 you asked the question, 'How expensive urban properties been weighed and found wanting in that they have taken away millions of dollars annually from the world evangelism? How many aspiring men have been turned away in their efforts to raise support because of a building program?' — you don't really want me to answer those two questions, do you? You know how very strongly I feel about that. Too, this letter has already gone too long, but I wanted to give you my opinions regarding your fine book. You are *right on target.* Please don't let anyone deter you in your desire to see our Lord's church multiply . . . one that He gave His precious blood for. If there is any way that I can help you in this please call on me. . . . I want very much that my co-workers and my elders read your good book. Please find enclosed a check . . . "

(E.J.L., Jan. 11, 1982)

"You bring truth to the statement that all who desire to live godly will suffer persecution. Jesus warned us to beware when all speak well of you. What I fear most though is that the alarm will not sound loud enough and we'll find ourselves as a people unable to meet needs and effect the positive changes so necessary in the troubling days ahead."

(L.A., Texas, Jan., 1982)

APPENDIX
— A —

The following text may serve as a basis for a descriptive brochure.

A Statement On . . .

HOW THINGS ARE SET IN ORDER

The metroplex community (or church) of Christ is governed by a group of directors which constitutes a presbytery or eldership. These biblically-qualified and ordained men administrate the responsibilities of the church in this city area. Each assembly has a teacher or elder who assists with teaching, correcting and exhorting. The elders meet each week (or more frequently when occasion requires) to handle church business, oversee and distribute church funds and adjudicate problems.

The church meets each week on a regularly appointed day, Sunday, the Lord's Day, and commend it as a day to worship and be with God's people. On a regular basis (usually once a month) all of the brothers and sisters in the entire fellowship gather together in a large rented facility.

This methodology has allowed us to invest more of our resources in leadership, to grow without having to build buildings, to preserve the close fellowship of a small church, and to accomplish the goals of a larger church.

Our concept and goal, in addition to the normal responsibilities, involves providing each household head in the fellowship with a close one-to-one relationship with an elder (shepherd). It is within this context that personalized teaching, counseling and life-formation can most effectively take place. It also brings parents and children closer together in a teaching and learning experience. This has consistently resulted in the emergence of new leaders who in many cases will progress and become full-time teachers, evangelists or shepherds.

Throughout the metroplex area, small home groups consisting of an elder or teacher, a few fathers and their families gather regularly for fellowship, worship, teaching, recreation and joyful 'family' occasions. These home groups provide the opportunity for families and individuals to walk out the Christian life in a context of strong support from others who are closely associated with them.

In addition to the home groups there are others who congregate in buildings that have been erected specifically for church assemblies. These congregations are usually somewhat larger, and are frequently assisted by several overseers in addition to teachers and evangelists. On Sundays, each group (whether in homes or church buildings) comes together as a congregation. These meetings are centered in teaching the Bible, fellowship, the breaking of bread (the Lord's Supper) and in prayers. In turn, these smaller groups assemble together once a month for a culminative celebration of worship, evangelism and fellowship which encompasses all of the people in the fellowship throughout the city area.

We are not a denomination with human traditions and dogmas; we recognize no authority other than Christ, and no church or ecclesiastical organization higher than the elders which are appointed 'in every city.' Various members of our community of believers in Christ maintain an active dialogue with many other local ministers and church leaders. We highly value these relationships and seek to broaden our participation in the evangelization of the world within our generation.

Benefits of the Shepherding Approach To Evangelism and Edification

1. Provides intimate shepherd-sheep relationship (John 10:1-14).

2. Shepherds truly care for the individual needs of each member's personal life.

3. Enables all shepherds of entire city area (metroplex) to counsel together without any barriers of congregations in same area.

4. Enables all shepherds of the city to participate jointly in study, in prayer, and in reaching combined decisions like the Jerusalem elders did (Acts 11:30).

5. Provides much stronger potential for support of foreign missions.

6. Frees much additional funds for supporting evangelists, pastors and teachers at home.

7. The heavy expense of purchasing real estate is eliminated, while utilizing existing facilities of homes and rented halls at much more economical rates.

8. Teaching the Bible to children is the main responsibility of the parents, thus strengthening the family unit while inciting more Bible study and discussion on a day-to-day basis.

9. Provides more places of assembly, giving more non-Christian neighbors an opportunity to become involved in Bible studies without the bias or prejudice that is often associated with an invitation for them to "go to church" which they understand to be a church building.

10. The occasional area-wide assemblies in a large facility provide fellowship and strength needed to supplement the smaller home assemblies.

11. Younger men have greater awareness of their need for leadership participation, and they can much more easily identify with the teacher or preacher in this

setting as a pattern within reach for their imitation.

12. As the Metro church grows in numerical strength, the large assemblies in prominent public buildings will attract attention of the citizens, and well-known evangelists can be invited to preach which will attract the brethren.

13. New places of assembly (in homes) can be arranged without a consideration of the financial abilities of those being taught.

14. The ministry support arrangement enables the instructor to benefit directly from the material things of those he instructs, like the shepherd who lives directly from the material things of those he nurtures, keeps and directs in his flock (John 10:1-14).

15. The new convert receives strong encouragement to go and teach others what he has been taught (1 Tim. 2:2). This assures his own continued growth, the growth of the kingdom in general, and will certainly assure his own continued faithfulness.

16. Any faithful man can easily see how he may reach the degree of fruitfulness to become fully supported in his ministry within a relatively short period of time.

17. The number of 'pulpits' opened through this method can accomodate the needs of scores and even hundreds of capable ex-preachers and ex-teachers in getting back into actively spreading the Word.

18. Transportation is greatly reduced, with more assemblies in the immediate neighborhoods.

19. Elders as shepherds watch in behalf of souls; they are unburdened as manager of big church finance, administration of large real estate properties, etc. Worries about losing members to other congregations is practically eliminated, and the rush to 'keep up with other congregations' building programs' is non-existent.

20. There is no way to outgrow facilities. Simply meet in more homes and rent more or larger halls. If a church

is growing as it should and as it did in the first century, this is the only way the crowds could be handled.

21. Provides opportunities for frequent fellowship around a table feast of love.

22. Eliminates the concept that the church building is the church.

23. Conforms to every known biblical and practical principle (Acts 2:46; 5:42 etc.).

— B —

The following letter may serve as a suggestion for communicating to individuals who need to be re-enlisted to active service.

METROPLEX COMMUNITY (CHURCH) OF CHRIST

Phone   City Address

To Those Who
Seek A Better Life
Greetings in the Name of Jesus!

We're building an army, an army for God to fight His battles. This call may not be for you or for your family at all. In fact, if you are now serving God and are happily situated, this is not your summons.

Misfits and discontented people. Maybe deeply in debt who see no way out. People in distress who feel they have nothing financially or perhaps otherwise to give. Maybe one time active, but now on a shelf or turned out to pasture, or unable to find a satisfying place of service. You may not be called to live in the open fields or caves of the earth, nor like the men who volunteered to serve in David's army will you be compelled to hide from your brothers and friends who dwell safely and securely . . . "All those who were in distress or in debt or discontented gathered around him, and he became their leader. About 400 men were with him" (2 Sam. 22:1-2).

170

We know there are many more than 400 men of such description in this troublous time in this metro area, men who have not found a place where they fit in. It has been reported that there are more members of churches of Christ who are NOT serving nor faithfully attending, than there are who do. And it is not uncommon to look out in the pews in many of the congregations and see several ex-preachers and ex-teachers. If our figures are correct, the potential is 50 times 400, or upward of 20,000 soldiers of Christ who are inactive or AWOL. All these are now being called back into active service for our Wonderful King Jesus!

The aim? Not to build another church building nor to settle down in any way that will be comfortable and relaxing from a material point of view. We shall be pilgrims on the way to a better land, perhaps meeting in hundreds of homes and rented halls with a firm resolve that resources God may entrust to us will go toward helping the downtrodden and toward preaching the gospel to a lost world. With the gospel message we shall be unyielding; with opinions and methods there is a vast unknown, wherever and however God may lead.

And this company will grow. These outcasts are expected to be transformed and a new outlook will come to them like to Elijah when he had all but given up. The numbers will grow, like the first century church grew when it was not limited by barriers of race, by economic or social standards nor by the walls of any building. Will you come and hear more of these dreams based on the most simple ideas from the Book of the first century? You are invited to call the number above or write.

Sincerely Yours,
(Signed)

— C —

This letter may serve as an invitation to an existing assembly in the same locality to consider working as one church united under one eldership.

**A PROPOSAL
TO THE ZAMORANO HOUSE ASSEMBLY**

In view of the liberty allowed by the Scriptures that enables the church of our Lord in any given city to assemble for worship under one leadership (eldership) in multiple places of assembly on the Lord's Day, and in acknowledgment of this arrangement being now commonly practiced and accepted among the churches of Christ, with a motivation of more effective evangelism and greater unity among Christians in the greater Dallas/Fort Worth area, the following proposals are humbly submitted for your prayerful consideration and acceptance:

1. Recognize and accept all Christians who prefer or find it more convenient to participate in worship assemblies in homes on the Lord's Days, and assist in developing multiple-place assemblies under one eldership in the metroplex, both in and out of church-owned properties.

2. Seek to unite under one leadership with other existing congregations in the city area, without thoughts or plans to assemble each week at one time and place.

3. Consider all potential elders' names to be placed before the congregation for appointment, some accepting the particular concern and responsibility in oversight in "away from the church building" assemblies. This would constitute the same relationship as other elders may now occupy with reference to other phases or groups such as finance, deaf assemblies, Spanish assemblies, etc. Accept all elders as one group for overseeing the urban ekklesia, body, or community of believers.

4. Re-examine the use of any church name that would tend to identify the whole church with one street address or location within the city.

5. Contributions from all assemblies of the church will be carried each week for deposit in a common treasury, a comparable portion of which will be expended in the propagation of each several ministry and so far as possible, according to their needs expressed to the eldership.

6. Christians in various groups will be encouraged to visit each others' meetings if they wish to do so, and all will meet together from time to time as one body in a large place such as a rented hall or coliseum for fellowship, worship and encouragement.

For further consultation, please contact us at the address given above.

[Note: A form is available by which a request is made by a group which wants to be recognized as a part of the community of believers in the city. Write to Star Bible and ask for form "Request for Recognition." Another "House Church Weekly Report Form" is available, designed to be brought each week to the elders from all the house churches including a record of attendance, baptisms, visitors, contributions, suggestions, needs, etc.]

— D —

The following work description of the messenger of the church may be adapted for use in any metropolis where the saints may already be assembling.

(NAME) ANGEL OF THE CHURCH IN THE CITY OF _____

Whereas (name) has been uniquely suited and trained in heart, mind and spirit to serve in what God may have reserved for him as the most significant work in the Kingdom in modern times, this resume' of proposed labors is laid out after earnest prayer and meditation. May (name), the angel or messenger of the church, and all the saints that may become involved in these efforts, be strengthened in accepting and in accomplishing what is proposed to the glory of His praise.

I. LOCATE GROUPS OF DISCIPLES WHO WILL UNITE AS ONE LOCAL CHURCH OF (CITY)

A. Find and/or assist in developing HOUSE CHURCHES and other assemblies under one eldership, and encourage appointment of as many elders as become qualified and recognized by their group(s).

B. Find STRUGGLING OR SMALL GROUPS which have no overseers and invite them to join together into one. Several are already in the metro area that have shown interest. A letter has already been drafted.

C. Find CONGREGATIONS which already have overseers who would be willing to plan their work in conjunction with other elders in this metro area in developing one united community of believers in Jesus Christ under one leadership.

II. COORDINATION OF ALL GROUPS AS ONE COMMUNITY OF SAINTS

Without interruption of present regular assemblies, all would agree to meet together occasionally as appointed by the elders, perhaps three to six times a year, in a large convention hall for fellowship, evangelism and a celebration of praise, growth, thanksgiving and joy. This coordination and cohesion would be accomplished by these means under the careful supervision of the elders:

A. Weekly bulletin mailed to each family, carrying news, Bible instruction, announcements, listing of all participating groups (with time, place, teacher, etc. of each one).

B. Outlines of Bible studies and sermons to be taught each week at the Lord's Day assemblies and at all other Bible talks, etc. These outlines could be sent out as part of the weekly bulletin, or in separate communications to the group leader.

C. Appointment of two trusted servants in each group to be responsible for delivery of weekly contributions into the common treasury of the church in (City Name).

D. Approval of new groups to be added and their leaders.

E. The use of any one stereotyped name would be discouraged so as to avoid being denominated or sectarianized.

III. A PLAN FOR ALL GROUPS COMPRISING THE WHOLE CHURCH IN (CITY NAME) FOR MEETING AT ONE TIME AND PLACE IN ONE GREAT ASSEMBLY

Such a plan would include such appointments as:

A. Evangelist(s) for the occasion.

B. Selection of suitable facility.

C. Advertising to saturate the entire metro area.

D. Worship and work details to accomodate the crowds.

E. Follow-up procedures to teach and help all newcomers and visitors, designed to involve them all in a regular "house church" assembly and Bible talk session.

These large gatherings would not be on a regular weekly basis, but would occur from three to six times annually, as directed by the elders.

The following newspaper advertisement has been used effectively to find believers who are isolated who may be seeking fellowship.

IN THE FIRST
TWO CENTURIES OF CHRISTIANITY
THE CHURCH MET IN HOUSES

OF ITS MEMBERS. During this time, the religion of Jesus Christ spread more rapidly than it has in any period of its history. All the city of Jerusalem, where Jesus built His church, was soon "filled" with His teachings (Acts 5:28). Within 50 years, the message of Christ's good news had gone out to "all creation" in the world . If you would like help in starting an assembly in your own house, or if you would like to know if one may already exist near you, write to the church in D/FW, Box 181220, Ft. Worth, 76118. Please enclose a stamped envelope with your house address. There is **No charge.**

— E —

What Prominent Leaders In The Church
Are Saying

These thoughts and statements reflect general evaluations of the condition of the church today, and are from men, for the most part, who had no connection with or awareness of the writing of this book.

"A church exists only as it relates to missions."

Ed Matthews
Abilene Christian University
ACU Missions Training Seminar, 1981

"We have become so congregationally autonomous that we have become provincial . . . we don't know what's going on outside our local church."

Prentice Meador
Springfield, Missouri
ACU Missions Training Seminar

"If the church of Christ does not exist in your community you should start one! And it is possible for it to begin meeting in your very own home . . . if the church in its true form already exists there, then beginning a new congregation might not be advisable."

Cline Paden
Director
Sunset School of Preaching
"How To Set Up A Church In Your Home"

"We are considering oversight for small ethnic groups, young in the faith, here in New York City. There is only one group of elders in the city and these brethren desperately need the experience and leadership this would provide."

Kieth Mitchell
Minister & Elder

"The church is not a place, but a people. It is not a facility but a fellowship. It is not a building but a body. The early church did not have buildings as we know them today (Rom. 16:5; Philemon 2). They met in homes. I believe in small groups. They are biblical. The Greek word for house, *oikos*, appears at least 19 times, and there are 9 references to times when believers worshiped and/or were taught in a home (Acts 2:2-4, 46; 5:42; 10:24-48; 16:25-34; 16:40; 20:17-20; 21:8-14; 28:30, 31). The home was utilized as a place of worship."

Charles Sattenfield
(Firm Foundation, Jan. 1980, p. 73)

"The growth rate of our BIG congregations is very poor with *very* few exceptions. Small-group dynamics worked in the first two or three centuries and will work today. Cathedral-itis, Program-itis, Bigness-itis, and Sanctuary-itis are killing us."

Jim Bob Jarrell
Letter, February 13, 1981

"I have no problem with such arrangements nor do I share with brother ____'s contention that the concept is unscriptural."

Ron Smotherman, Evangelist
Smithfield, Texas

"We have made but little progress in the last ten years with all our beautiful buildings and fast talk. . . Our use of "Church of Christ" in the fullness of truth cannot be wrong, but in some respects we have gone beyond truth and both legalized and denominationalized the name. . . . The souls in your community are, before God, your responsibility. If you and your elders are not sufficiently interested to help reach your own neighbors, don't blame me if I keep trying."

Jimmie Lovell, editor
Action — Jan. & Feb., 1981

"These can be led by elderships in each church building location, or *there can be one total eldership per city,* or (temporarily at least) a church without elders."

Bill Patterson, editor
Christian Bible Teacher, Dec. 1980, p. 606
"Church Growth"

"Body-life programs are killing the church — drawing our focus on ourselves inwardly instead of looking outward to the field of the world."

George Gurganus
Abilene Christian University
ACU Missions Training Seminar '81

"The church at _____ has a budget for this year of $171,000, of which only $100 is marked for missions."

(Name Withheld)

"It is now evident that a major correction is needed. The 1965 Almanac counts (of churches of Christ, 15,000; members, 2,500,000) were highly exaggerated . . . there are 12,706 local congregations with a total membership of 1,206,799. There are only 200 'main-line' congregations with a membership of 500 or more, only 24 with 1,000 or more, only 4 with 2,000 or more. The average congregation has only 100 membership (Mac Lynn's census).

"Religious census data on many local communities indicates that there are more members of the church of Christ who are *not* identified with any local congregation than there are who are."

Dr. Flavil Yeakley, Jr.
"Why Churches Grow", 1981

"Even a superficial review of our present patterns shows that we are in serious trouble. It is simple mathmatics — when our gains are less than our losses, the church is proportionally in decline."

Gerald Paden
Firm Foundation, Feb. 24, 1981
"Church Growth—A Critical Need"

"It doesn't make a bit of sense to throw the seed inside four walls then wonder why a world out there isn't paying any attention! There's only one way to win folks, and that's to get out amongst them and give your life. That's the way Jesus did it. That's the only way. There is no short cut."

Landon Saunders
"Heartbeat" Radio Evangelist
"Feeling Good About Being A
Christian," Tape 1, 1980

"We probably spend six dollars per member per year on foreign evangelism, but we cannot get the job done and spend only six dollars per member per year."

J. C. Bailey
South India Newsletter
Dec. — Jan., 1981

"Early Christians met in their homes to worship God (Rom. 16:5; 1 Cor. 16:19; Col. 4:15; Philemon 2). We should remember that the early church, as recorded in the New Testament did not own property, and yet they were very successful in preaching the Gospel to the whole world (Col. 1:23)."

Lynn Yocum
"How To Become A Christian And Establish The Church of Christ In Your Community," pp. 9-10

"Areas where there are many Christians and effective leaders could use a combination of cell-meetings during the week, and central meeting places, in which the whole church can come together. Both are essential, I believe, to the best functioning of the body as a whole, especially in larger congregations. Members need both the intimacy and mutual sharing of small groups and the dynamics of large groups to maintain a balanced sense of spiritual perspective."

Glover Shipp
Belo Horizonte, Brazil
"House Church," Firm Foundation
Oct. 25, 1977

"We have been in the Philippines for 10 years and have been in the process of developing the 'House-church'."

Charles Smith, Minister
Arkansas

"Difficulties with the principles advanced in this book may be experienced in implementation, but not in biblical soundness. An energy shortage, an economic squeeze, or a cessation of government tax exemption to churches could force the acceptance of the alternatives stated herein."

Dr. John Bailey
Hurst, Texas

— F —

WHAT OTHERS ARE DOING

It is not the intention in this section to give endorsement or approval to doctrinal positions held by the groups which we shall review, nor to the books recently published which we shall cite. The purpose is to demonstrate that many of the distinctive biblical principles outlined in the first edition of our book have been written about and implemented for quite a long while, unknown to this writer at the time of his first writing in 1981. Except for the three isolated instances cited in our first edition, we were unaware of other current efforts, and *none* of these that we now mention had come to our attention. Taking the New Testament alone, we tried to envision the early church's function and growth, supposing there were few others, if any who practice these things today. After reading my book, however, one reader would say, "Have you heard about a group at a certain place already practicing these things?" Another would respond, "There is a book that sounds much the same as you wrote; have you seen _____ (gives title)?" When we thought we were pioneers in the field, we discovered others had covered the same territory and plowed the same ground as early as sixty years ago. A brief description of some of these other works now follows.

Dr. Cho of Korea

In 1958, Dr. Paul Yonggi Cho had a tent mission in Seoul with no members. Today he has the largest congregation in the world. His growth pattern statistics are: 1958, 150 members; 1959, 300; 1960, 600; 1973, 18,000; 1979, 100,000; 1980, 120,000; 1981, 150,000 members. After his book was written in 1981 *(Successful Home Cell Groups)* a newspaper reporter compared his 350,000 member church with the "puny" membership of 23,000 in the First Baptist Church of Dallas, Texas.

Dr. Cho does not work alone. He has 320 associate ministers, 400 office workers, 120 missionaries and 20,000 unpaid "lay leaders." He explained on a recent tour that the secret to church growth is using all the members in teaching in their homes because people "won't come to church, but they will come to a neighbor's house." He believes "America is where it could happen because American people have big vision. If they can visualize men on the moon, they can visualize anything." He is constantly training others to minister, so they will "put me out of a job."

"The traditional models of chruch growth and leadership simply do not work on such a large scale," he wrote in the introduction of his book (page V). He warns that many who attempt home "cell" meetings do not succeed because they disregard certain important principles. Evidently his plan is working better than any other in the world, if we could measure by the 10,000-plus home Bible studies his members conduct each week. When he renounced arrogance and personal ambition as disastrous and learned to delegate more responsibility to involve more people, this marked the beginning of his success in numeric growth. Seven distinct problems were corrected as they arose, termed by their leader as "Satan's counter-attack" (see pages 34ff).

These home meetings began as an effort to destroy "depersonalization of human beings" who felt alienated, lonely and aimless. Dr. Cho described his church as the "smallest and the biggest" church in the world because the one church is a conglomerate community of members in small groups looking out for each other. He sets goals, trains and motivates people to dream (Prov. 29:18), serve one another, and plan ahead.

The "Local Church" of Watchman Nee And Witness Lee

Watchman Nee (1903-1972) started a "house church" of the Plymouth Brethren type in Foochow, China, in 1922. In the late 20's he wrote a book, *The Spiritual Man,* in which he gave his views on the body, soul and spirit. Ten years later he published *Concerning Our Missions* (later re-named *The Normal Christian Church Life*) in which he spelled out the positions he had begun to take: (1) The church ought to be united—denominationalism is a sin. (2) There is to be only one church within each geographic area and it must not be associated with any other church. (3) All believers should break away from denominations and join with or establish "local churches."

Witness Lee came into the "Little Flock" movement in the 1930's and "came into the local church" in 1932. By 1940, Lee became a close associate of Watchman Nee and added his own flair for organization which Nee lacked. They worked together in Shanghai until 1948, the year that marked a turning point in the Church's organizational practices and a system of hierarchical control. Nee appointed Lee as autocratic leader of the Little Flock of Taiwan. Membership in the Local Church outside the USA in 1976 was about 35,000, with an added 7,000 in the United States and Canada. Lee's influence extends far beyond the membership of the Local Church, however, through his many books and pamphlets issued from Living Stream, Inc. in Anaheim, California. Witness Lee is president of this organization. In 1978 a significant split occurred in the local Church headquarters when more than 40 members of the Anaheim congregation withdrew. The Local Church is at a critical stage in its history with lawsuits pending due to external challenges, and with mounting internal controversy.

Witness Lee's mystical and sensuous theology of subjectivity has brought him and his movement into basic conflict with outsiders. Lee emphasizes that Local Church members have a superior "subjective Christ" while people in denominational bodies have only an inferior "objective Christ."

Our purpose here is not to review doctrinal deviances, however, but rather to show a significant point of similarity with our views expressed in 1981. This has to do with the concept of only one church in each locality. The "Local Church" derives its name from Nee's and Lee's teaching of "local ground." They teach that according to the New Testament there is no reference to a church whose jurisdiction is smaller than a city. This is considered to be no mere happenstance, but rather a divine principle. Thus each Local Church is named after its city: "the Church in Anaheim," "the Church in Antioch," etc. (See numerous references including Lee's *The Practical Expression of the Church* pp 57-58, 68-71, 92, 107). Watchman Nee's book, *Further Talks on the Church Life*, discusses in detail the principle of one church in a city locality and the church assemblies in many homes in chapters one and two (taught first in Chinese in 1922, p. 48; spoken and published in 1950, p. 5; copyrighted by Stream Publishers, Los Angeles, 1974). Nee pointed out two "great mistakes": (1) People desire to have a church bigger than a city or a locality, or on the other hand, (2) people desire to have a church smaller than the city or the locality (pages 40-43). Notice from page 42: "There must have been over 10,000 brothers in Jerusalem, and they might have been divided into 100 houses for meetings (we do not know the definite number). As houses of this kind are smaller than the city, smaller than the locality and smaller than Jerusalem, they are not sufficient to become the units of the churches. Therefore, if you add one hundred houses together, they do not become one hundred churches. In the Bible, there is only the church at Jerusalem in the single number." Similar expressions occur in Witness Lee's, *The Practical Expression of the Church,* 1970. The Stream Publishers, pages 23-32, 68-71.

Book: *Social Aspects of Early Christianity*

Dr. Abraham J. Malherbe, Professor of New Testament Criticism and Interpretation at the Divinity School of Yale University, has written a second and enlarged edition of his book first published in 1977 by Louisiana State University Press. In this edition published in 1983 by Fortress Press, chapter four is added from a formerly published paper in Oslo: "Hospitality and Inhospitality in the Church." Chapter three entitled "House Churches and Their Problems" is as complete and carefully researched as any on the subject we have seen. He is convinced that as a church grew in a particular locality, more than one house church would be formed but that these separate groups "were not viewed as separate churches." In support of this he cites Jerusalem as one church, and also Paul's "relating presbyters, or bishops, to cities rather than to individual groups (Acts 14:23; 20:17; Titus 1:5)." Even though Paul knew of several groups in a locality, he wrote only one letter to "the church" there (e.g. Romans), concluding that "the individual house churches would together have represented the church in any one area" (page 70).

Book: *By This Shall All Men Know*

Boyce Mouton has written (1979) concerning the supreme mark of *love* as the distinguishing trait of God's people. Mouton's book of 102 pages was published by College Press and circulates principally among the independent Christian Church fellowship of believers.

In answering the question, "What is the church?", he responds in part that it consists of a single church in each city — "the word 'churches' is never used in the Scriptures to refer to the Christians in a single city" (page 34). He continues: "There may have been a hundred 'house churches' in Jerusalem but every reference to them is always in the singular." The author gives a rather lengthy discourse in defense of the concept of a "City Church" (pp 35-39).

He feels the worst investment the traditional Christian Community makes, and yet the one thing it feels "most safe in owning", may be the church building (pp 60-62).

Book: The First Urban Christians: The Social World of the Apostle Paul

Wayne Meeks in this volume of 299 pages has recaptured a sense what it was like to be a Christian in the first century. He has sought to give an understanding of the setting, the community, and the practices of the disciples of Paul's day. His search into ancient history, sociology and anthropology illuminates the well-known material found in the New Testament concerning this "new religious movement."

Of particular interest in our study is chapter 3, "The Formation of the Ekklesia." He focuses on the household and how the house became the meeting place for Christians, and touches on the rich biblical language that spoke of Christians as belonging to a very specially related family (pp 84-88). Yale University Press, publisher, 1983.

Book: The Master's Plan For Making Disciples

Win Arn and Charles Arn teamed up in 1982 to bring out this 176-page book published by Church Growth Press in Pasadena, California. The main thrust of the Arns is to show from the Bible how every member of the church can be effective in evangelism. It is said by one reviewer to "unshackle the laity for effective involvement in the Great Commission." Dr. Win Arn is President and founder of the Institute for American Church Growth, has authored several books on the theme, and has produced ten color films in the field of church growth.

Book: Discipling — The Multiplying Ministry

Milton Jones discusses in this book not only what it means to be a disciple, but also gives helpful information on how to imitate Jesus' strategy of preparing a nucleus of disciples who would equip others to multiply all over the world. Dr. Jones is evangelist at the Northwest Church of Christ in Seattle, and also directs the Northwest School of Discipleship. Joe Barnett writes in the foreword: "If the principles of this book are applied, we will come to the year 2,000 many times our present numerical and spiritual strength." Star Bible & Tract Corp., Ft. Worth, Texas. 1982. 155 pages.

Book: *Upward, Inward, Outward!*

This book by Milton Jones is a course in maturing disciples in Christ — growing in relationships with God, with our brothers and sisters, and with people outside the body of Christ. Published in 1984 by Star Bible Publications, Ft. Worth, Texas. 64 pages.

Book: *The Early Church*

Gene Edwards wrote this provocative 243-page book in 1974 and it was published by Christian Books of Goleta, California. It purports to be a history of the first century church, written to "stir young men's hearts with the glory of what the church once was and should be—can be—in their lifetime. Edwards believes the true story of the early church is virtually unknown to Christians of the twentieth century. He feels the present system cannot be reformed because it is too far off course, and therefore it should be abandoned. He writes: "A 'pastor', standing behind a pulpit preaching sermons to a group of people seated in pews in a building with stained glass windows has absolutely no Scriptural justification whatsoever. You will never find such a scene in all first century literature" (Pages 1-3). He speaks of a church building as a "coffin", reminds his readers that the principle place of assembling was in homes, and that such homes all over the city comprised "the church, united, one, in love, inseparable, and glorious" (pp 49-50). "The early church never owned property" (p. 62).

Reviewers concluded, "The church as you have never experienced it, but the way you have always known it should be."

Book: *The Master Plan of Evangelism*

My friend Jim Bobo first gave me a copy of this outstanding book in 1982 while we were attending an evangelism seminar in California. Robert Coleman wrote this little volume in 1963. It had gone through its 35th printing by 1980 — over 700,000 copies. Published by Spire, this little 126-page book contends that (1) Men were Christ's method, (2) He required obedience, (3) He showed them how to live, and (4) He expected results. It focuses not so much on the actions of Jesus as on the underlying principles that consistently determined what His action would be in any given situation.

Note: For prices and availability on books in this section, contact Star Bible Publications, Ft. Worth, TX 76118.

Index of Scripture References

Index of Persons